chic bags

www.stmartins.com

Publisher: Christophe Savouré
Editor: Gaëlle Guilmard
Art director: Laurent Quellet et Thérèse Jauze
Production: Florence Bellot
Photography: Frédéric Lucano
Model: Marine Klein
Stylist: Lélia Deshayes
Book design and layout: Iris Glon
Ilustrations: Iwona Séris

Library of Congress Cataloging-in-Publication Data Available Upon Request

ISBN-10: 0-312-37074-1
ISBN-13: 978-0-312-37074-9

First published in France by Fleurus

First U.S. Edition: July 2007

10 9 8 7 6 5 4 3 2 1

Marie Enderlen-Debuisson / Caroline Laisné

chic bags

22 Handbags, Purses, Totes and Accessories to Make

St. Martin's Griffin New York

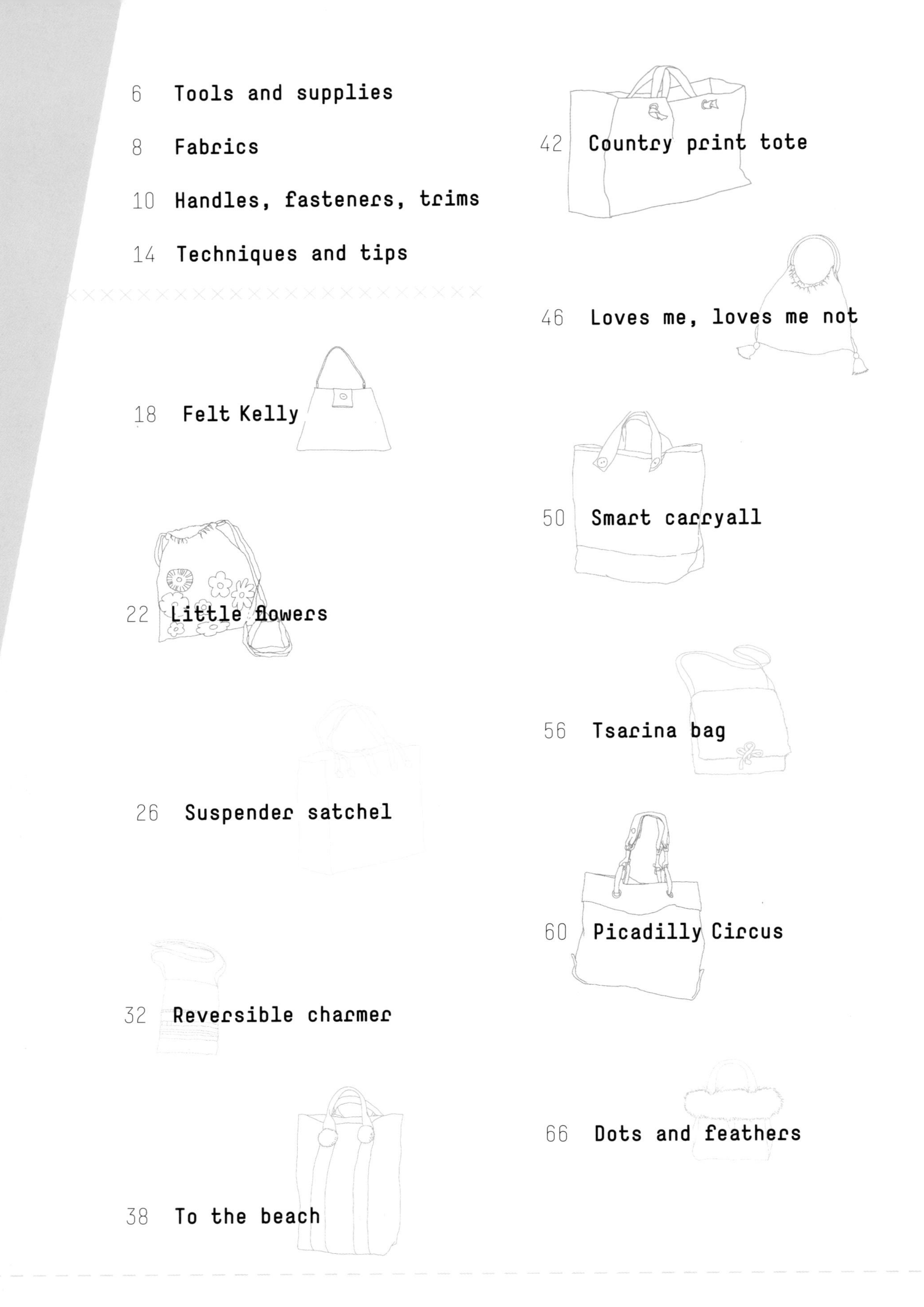

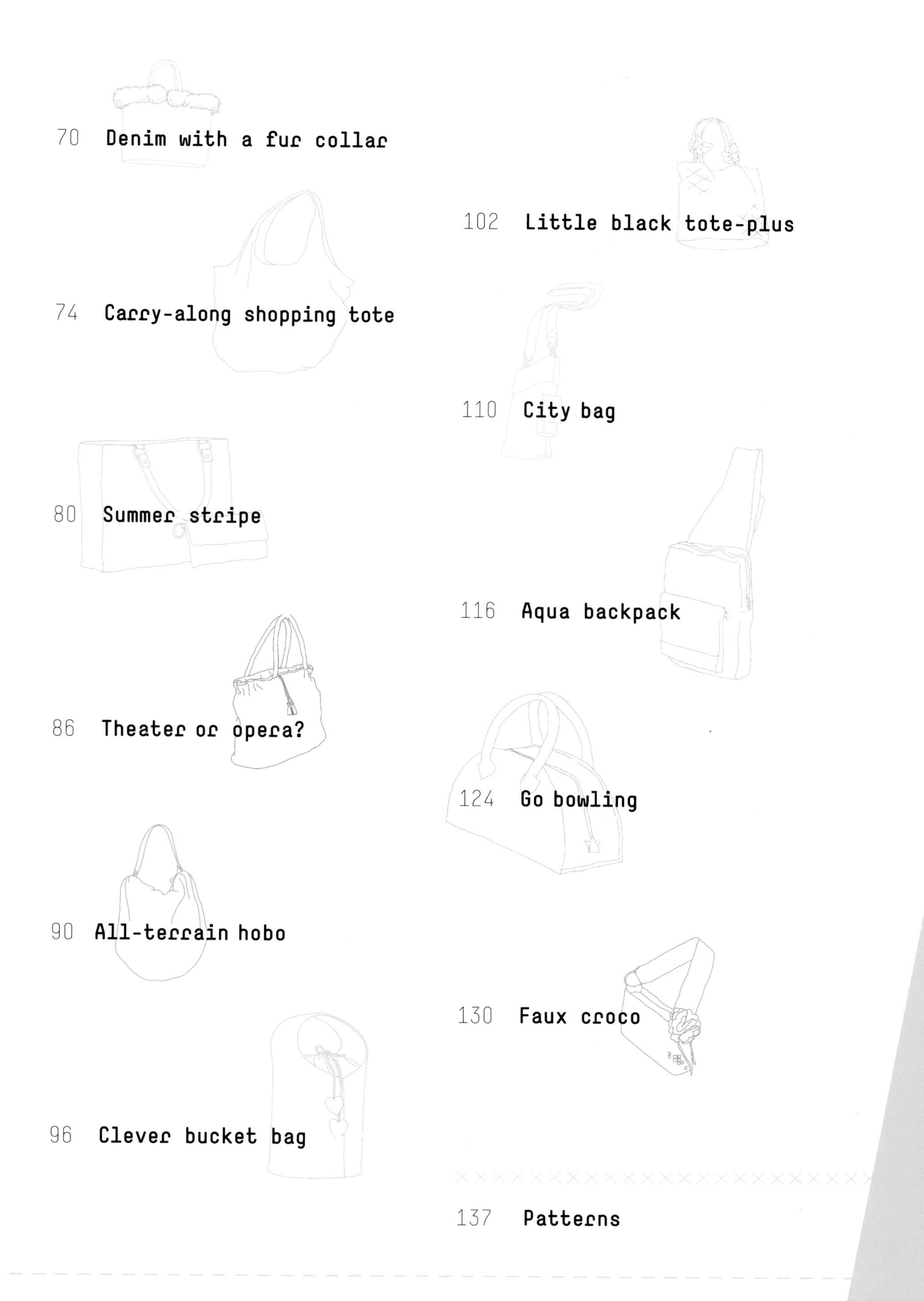

Tools and supplies

The bags in this book were assembled with a sewing machine, with the exception of two that are made of heavy felt. Besides a machine, you will need an iron and ironing board so you can press the fabric as you work. Here are the other tools you should have on hand.

Needles and pins

- Keep hand-sewing needles (sharps) in various sizes in your work area; for some bags you'll need a leather needle (with a sharp, triangular point). To add embroidered details, you'll need embroidery needles (with sharp points) and tapestry needles (with blunt points) to use with embroidery floss and pearl cotton threads.
- Choose a machine needle of the right size and type for the fabric you are using. Sizes 60 to 75 for lightweight fabric, and sizes 100 to 120 for heavier fabric. There are also leather needles for sewing machines; they may work well for very thick materials but test the results before doing an entire seam—they are very sharp and can cause some materials to tear along the stitching line.
- Straight pins are indispensible for securing the pieces of your project while you sew; use thin pins with lightweight fabric, thicker ones with heavier materials. The kind with round, colored heads are easy to see. Store your pins in a pincushion or in a magnetic container.
- Use a safety pin to guide a drawstring or cord through a casing—choose a size that you can feel with your fingers through the fabric layers.

Threads

- Whether you are sewing by machine or by hand, use polyester thread—it is less linty than cotton thread and also stronger.
- Use a contrasting cotton thread to baste pieces together before sewing—especially if their contours require careful alignment. Once the permanent seams are sewn it is easy to see and remove the contrast thread. Use backstitches to secure the ends of basted seams—they're easier to remove than knots.
- For embroidered details, use six-strand embroidery floss (usually matte finish) or pearl cotton (twisted, with a slight sheen).

For measuring

- A flexible measuring tape is handy, especially for curves. Both cloth and plastic types work well.
- For precise measuring, using a flat ruler; use it also to guide your lines when marking the pieces on your fabric before cutting. An L-square will help you mark right angles. Quilters' rulers and other transparent rulers that are marked with gridded measurements are also handy.

For marking

- Nonpermanent felt-tip fabric marking pens are a good choice for marking most light-color fabrics (the inks are commonly blue or purple). There are two kinds: one that washes off and one that disappears after being exposed to the air for a few days. It is a good idea to test them on each fabric to be sure they do, indeed, disappear as expected. If you want the marks to be apparent for more than a day or so, use the wash-off pen so the marks will be there if your work is interrupted.
- To mark dark fabrics, use a white or pale color tailor's chalk or fabric marking pencil.

- On coated fabrics (like those used for tablecloths, rainwear, or tablecloth pads), mark discreetly on the wrong side of the fabric with a ballpoint pen. Use a ballpoint pen also on rubber or stencil Mylar used to stiffen or reinforce a bag.
- Use a drafting compass to mark circles.
- To draw paper patterns or mark out cardboard stiffeners, use regular lead pencil—and have an eraser and pencil-sharpener at hand.

For cutting

- To cut fabric, use good shears dedicated to that purpose; paper and other materials may dull their blades. Use small, sharp scissors to cut thread.
- Embroidery scissors with long, fine points are good for clipping thread close to the fabric surface and for trimming seam allowance in tight places.
- Pinking shears are a practical choice for quickly notching the seam allowance on curved edges (see fig. 12, page 15). Theyre also a good alternative to serging or zigzag-stitching for finishing the edges of fabric that doesn't ravel much.
- Use regular household shears for cutting coated or rubberized fabric, paper patterns, and stiffening materials such as stencil Mylar.
- To cut stiff, heavyweight materials like industrial felt or vinyl-coated fabric, use a rotary cutter. Replace the blade as needed to be sure it is always sharp, and use this tool carefully—the style with a finger guard and blade cover is a smart option. To protect your work surface, put the material to be cut on a self-healing cutting mat. Use an acrylic quilters' ruler to guide the blade while you cut.

Adhesives

- Contact cement will make a strong bond to support handles (purchase a small tube from a shoe-repair shop). Follow the directions on the package; the basic idea is to apply glue to both surfaces to be adhered, let the glue dry, and then press the glued areas together with your hands. There are other strong glues available at most crafts supply shops; check the labels to see which looks appropriate for the task at hand.
- Spray fabric adhesives are excellent choices for adhering batting to fabric and keeping it in place between the exterior and lining of a bag. They save time in preparing a quilted project too—faster than basting the layers together.

Things that make life easier

- A thimble makes hand sewing easier and protects your fingertip. Thimbles come in sizes; choose one that fits snuggly on your middle finger. The kind with a recessed tip will keep the needle end from slipping when pushed. Check out quilters' thimbles too; there are flexible and open-tipped styles that you may find comfortable.
- Use a seam ripper to quickly and safely pick out misplaced stitches and also to slice buttonholes.
- Brown kraft paper is ideal for making patterns; it's sturdy and not likely to rip. Graph paper is good for small pattern pieces; tracing paper for copying actual size patterns.
- Tissue paper can be used to prevent snag-prone or coated fabrics from getting caught in the feed dogs of your machine (see Tips, page 17). There are also temporary interfacings designed for this purpose; you can find them at most fabric shops.

Sewing essentials

Here are supplies to always have on hand; they aren't listed with the projects:

- Fabric shears
- Assorted needles
- Straight pins
- Seam ripper
- Tape measure
- Flat artists' or quilters' ruler

Fabrics

Cottons

Easy to work with, cottons come in an immense range of colors, patterns, and finishes. Choose a type suited to the style of the bag—appropriately soft or crisp, and as sturdy as needed.

Linens

Sturdy and appealingly natural, linens are appreciated for their durability. Even the finest linens feel more textured and stiffer than most cottons. They are also famous for their tendency to wrinkle—but that is part of their charm.

Fleece

Available in several weights, fleece is soft to the touch and soft in appearance. It's a knit, so use a ballpoint needle to avoid damaging its structure.

Industrial felt

Used in this book to identify a variety of heavyweight wool or wool/rayon blend felts. True industrial felt comes only in gray; there are diverse colors in other sturdy types of felt. These felts range in thickness from 1/4 inch to as much as 1 inch—but 1/2-inch thick is the maximum for a bag. Thinner qualities can be sewn by machine, thicker ones only by hand (use a leather needle). Cut straight edges with a rotary cutter guided by a ruler; use household shears to cut curved edges.

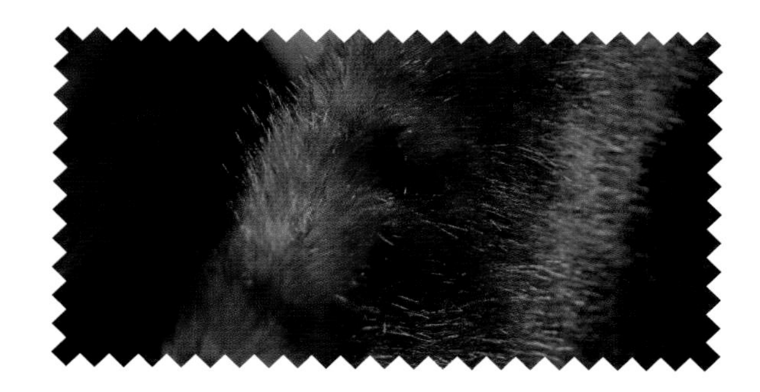

Fake fur

Professionals cut fake fur from the wrong side with a single-edge razor blade. Be sure to serge the edges of fake fur. Brush out your machine often to ensure the works don't fill with fur fibers.

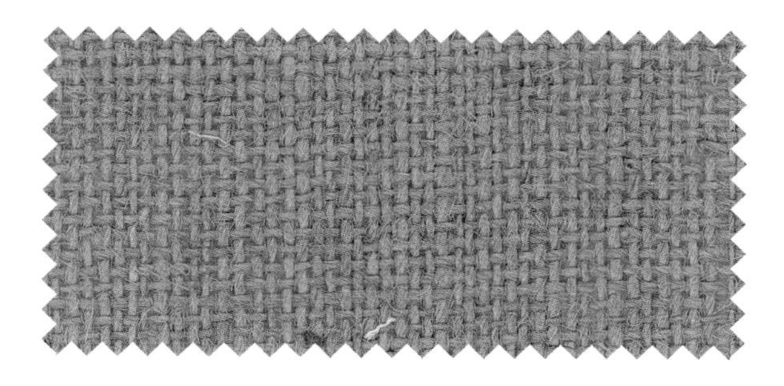

Burlap

Very sturdy, with a rustic character, burlap comes in natural jute color and in a variety of other hues. It's very linty and sheds while you work with it.

Home furnishings fabrics

Woven in wider widths than garment fabrics, these materials are generally durable and often have a protective surface finish. Reversible types such as mattress ticking and damask can be assembled so both faces show to create subtle contrasts or preclude the need for a facing.

Coated specialty fabrics

Many fabrics intended for use as tablecloths or rainwear as well as materials designed to keep scatter rugs from slipping or to protect a good table from spills are fine, if unexpected, choices for bags. While these materials don't ravel and require no edge finish, pins and misplaced stitches will leave permanent holes in them, so they should be test assembled with adhesive tape. They may be difficult to guide through your machine; a sandwich of tissue paper will help them move smoothly (see Tips, page 17).

Batting

Lightweight and medium-weight quilt batting can be slipped between the exterior and lining fabrics to give a soft, rounded quality to a bag. There are various polyester, cotton, wool, and silk options (and blends of these); choose one that feels compatible with your fabric and is not overly stiff.

Handles, fasteners, trims

Handles and straps

You can create handles by covering all manner of items with fabric: electrical cables, cotton cords, even plastic tubes that are used for plumbing or aquarium pumps. Plan on a length of about 14" (35 cm) for a handbag and about 40" (100 cm) for a shoulder bag.
Webbing and other sturdy ribbons also make excellent straps, especially the type worn over the shoulder and across the chest.
Sewing and crafts supply shops offer a large choice of readymade handles—look for plastic (including fake tortoiseshell), rattan, wood, and leather.
Don't hesitate to recycle handles and straps from bags you no longer use—or those you find in thrift shops. Consider also cloth and leather belts—even suspenders.

Closure options

Buttons and buttonholes

You'll find a nearly infinite choice of button materials: wood, horn, plastic, metal, mother-of-pearl. For buttons to be easily fastened through thick straps, there should be a space between the button and the bag. To create this space, slip a wooden cocktail pick or wooden matchstick under the button while you sew it on (fig. 1).

fig. 1

You can also cover plain buttons with fabric. Buy a kit for this and follow the directions on the package. Or choose a button with a shank, cut a circle of fabric larger than the button, sew long straight stitches around the edge by hand (see fig.13, page 16), and gather the edge of the fabric around the button shank (fig. 2).

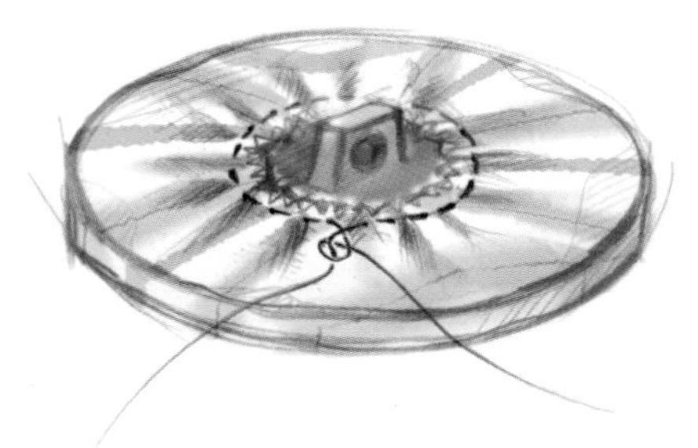

fig. 2

Refer to your sewing machine manual to mark buttonholes to correspond to the buttons: their length should be slightly longer than the diameter of the button. Sew them with a tight zigzag stitch or the automatic stitch on your machine; use a seam ripper to carefully cut them open.

fig. 3

fig. 4

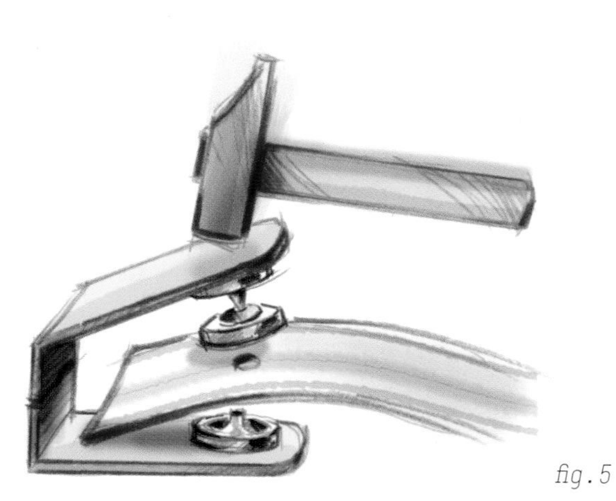

fig. 5

Gripper snaps

Gripper snaps come in a variety of diameters and with myriad cap colors and designs. You can purchase the tools for setting them at most sewing supply stores. Follow the directions in each project to position the snaps; then install them with the tools. Here's an overview of the method. Place your fabric over the protective plate and pierce the fabric by tapping the provided die with a small hammer (fig. 3). Install the male snap-setters in the flexible tool, position the two pieces of the male half of the snap in them, slide the fabric into the tool, and then tap the tool with the hammer to fix the snap in the fabric (fig. 4). Install the female half of the snap in the same way, using the appropriate parts of the tool (fig. 5).

You can also use a revolving rivet and snap setting tool (this looks something like pliers with a revolving wheel in one jaw); it is easy to use and can be adjusted for different size snaps and rivets. Whichever method you use, be sure to first take the time to mark the snap position correctly on each piece of fabric; make sure you mark and position the various components so the fabric and snaps will be correctly oriented when you are done. It's a good idea to do a test to be sure you understand the process—the pieced holes are permanent and once installed, the snaps are difficult to remove.

Magnets

Extremely strong, magnets provide a secure closure that is invisible on the outside of your bag. Install them face-to-face on the lining. Some types can be sewn on like buttons while others must be inserted in small pockets created for that purpose.

Zippers

Available in both metal and plastic, zippers come in a wide range of colors. You can buy standard lengths at any sewing store; some vendors sell zippers by the yard (or meter) but you must add the stops and slides to these yourself. The styles intended for blouses and jackets separate at both ends. Take your choice between the following techniques for sewing the zippers to your bag.

With concealed stitches - Along the edges where the zipper is to go, fold and then press ½" (1 cm) to the wrong side; then unfold the allowances. Working with one side at a time, pin the zipper, face down, to the right side of the allowance as shown below, aligning the foldline next to the zipper teeth (fig. 6). Baste the zipper tape to the allowance, then sew together on the foldline.

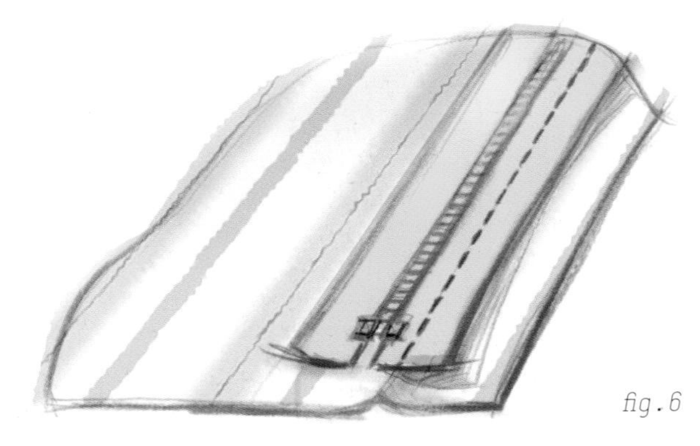

fig. 6

With visible stitches - Along the edges where the zipper is to go, fold and then press ½" (1 cm) to the wrong side. Place the zipper right side up. Place the fabric wrong side down on top of it, aligning each fold next to the zipper teeth (fig. 7). Pin, baste, and sew through all layers a short distance from each fold. If you are using a material that doesn't fray, it isn't necessary to fold under the allowance; just pin the edge next to the teeth.

fig. 7

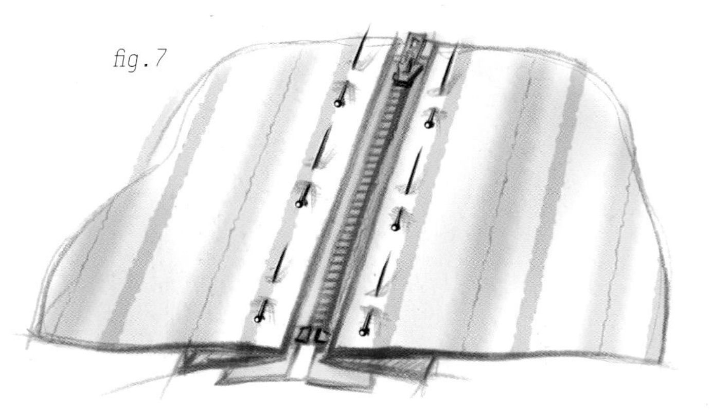

Whichever technique you choose, you'll need to have the zipper foot installed on your sewing machine. Also, as you sew, you'll need to move the zipper slide out of the way: stop sewing with the needle down, lift the zipper foot, move the slide, and then lower the foot and continue. Be sure to follow the directions for the bag you are making—sometimes you'll need to have the zipper open so that the bag can be turned right side out after the zipper is installed.

Velcro

This press-together closure tape is available in several widths and colors, in small rolls or by the yard. There are sew-on and self-adhesive types. As a rule of thumb, put the prickly half on the top layer of your project, the soft half on the bottom.

Linking gear

Grommets and eyelets

These circular metal bands provide a sturdy binding for holes of various sizes. Grommets are larger and have a front and back piece, eyelets are small and have only one piece. They are installed similarly to gripper snaps (see fig. 3 through 5, page 11). Be sure you mark your project properly and install both eyelets and grommets so that the smooth face is on the right side of your project and the stem that splits to grip the fabric is on the wrong side. Be careful to pierce holes of the correct size; if the hole is too big, the grommet or eyelet will not grip the fabric securely.

Rings

Crafts, notions, and even office supply shops offer a variety of rings—plastic, metal, wood. Some rings are closed, others are hinged (book rings), others have a lapped opening. Consider also using curtain rings, belt buckles, or key rings.

Snap hooks and double swivel rings

You can find these in crafts and hardware stores or recycle them from discarded bags or even a dog leash. Look also in sporting goods shops for interesting styles.

Ribbons, braids, cords and assorted trims

Trimmings shops offer an amazing variety of ribbons, braids, and cords in styles from very simple to marvelously sophisticated: you'll find pompons, fringes, bead- and sequin-embellished trims, tassels, twisted braids and cords, and plain and embroidered ribbons. Home furnishing trims have both the strength and flexiblity to work as straps. You can also combine them to make unique tassels or closures. You may also come across feather boas and real- or fake-fur stoles or collars that add interesting finishing touches.
These decorative trims may be sewn to your bag by machine or hand, or glued in place.

Techniques and tips

General directions

- When choosing which bag to make, read the directions all the way through to be sure you understand the process. The tips at the end of the projects contain important information too.
- If you are using several fabrics for the exterior of your bag, be sure they are of similar weight and thickness and drape compatibly.
- Before beginning a project, wash the fabrics and trims if possible; separate by color first. This will preclude different colors from running or rubbing off on each other later and ensure that your finished project won't shrink when laundered.
- Press all your fabrics carefully before marking and cutting.
- Many of the bags in this book require patterns, which are given on pages 138 through 160 (if they require enlarging, this is indicated in the section «Prepare the pieces» as well as on the pattern). Photocopy the patterns, or if you prefer, trace them if they are given actual size. If your pattern is given as a half-pattern, fold the fabric as shown in the layout diagram and place the dotted line of the pattern on the fold, then cut both layers of fabric at once (fig. 8); if the fabric is too stiff to fold, reverse the pattern along the dotted line (so the shape mirrors), drawing around each half and then cutting the whole.

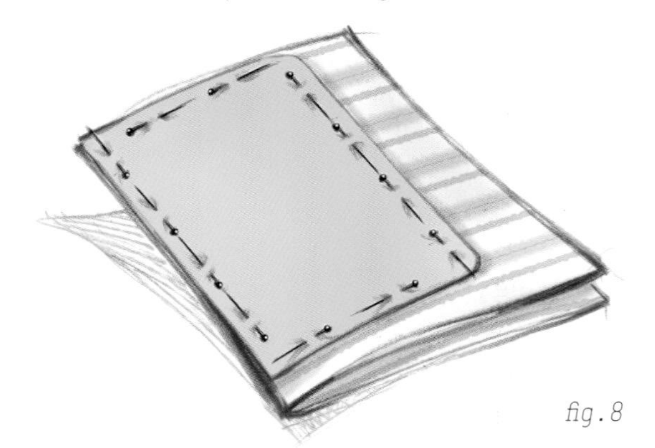

fig. 8

- Orient the patterns lengthwise on the straight grain of the fabric (parallel to the selvedge) (fig. 9). Match motifs and stripes on adjacent pieces.

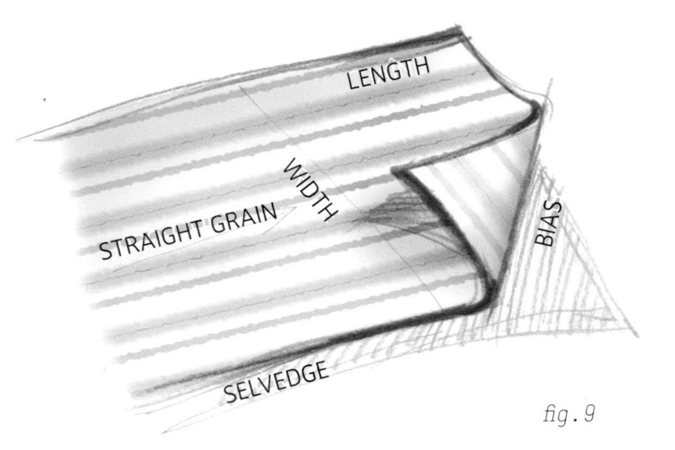

fig. 9

- You will need to add seam allowance around some of the given patterns. If this is the case, it is indicated in the section «Prepare the pieces».
- Even though the bags are lined, it's a good idea to finish the edges of all the pieces before sewing—do this with a serger or the zigzag stitch on your machine. However, if your fabric doesn't ravel, you may simply cut the pieces with straight or pinking shears, leaving a sufficient allowance for sewing. In particular, felt and vinyl-coated fabrics don't need to be serged or zigzagged.
- Before sewing, pin the pieces together; unless indicated otherwise, place the pins perpendicular to the seams, with their heads in the seam allowance (fig. 10). It's a smart idea to baste the seams before sewing by machine—the alignment will be better and the seams more accurate. Use

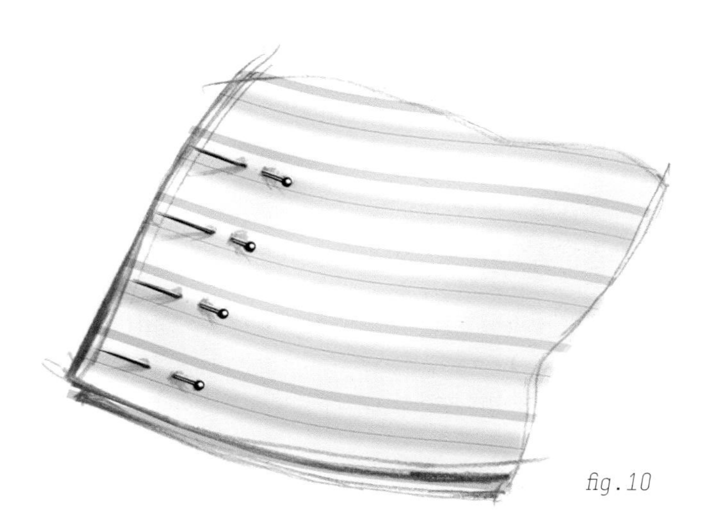

fig. 10

fig. 11

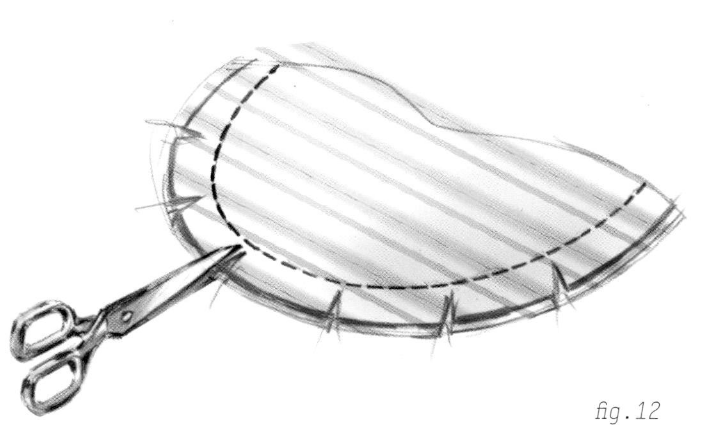

fig. 12

Terms at-a-glance

Foldline. *When you lay out the pieces for cutting, the dotted line on the half-patterns (given in the back of this book) should be placed on the fold of your fabric so that you can cut a complete shape through both layers.*
Seamline. *The line on which to sew.*
Seam allowance. *A margin between the edge of the fabric and the seamline; the directions in this book indicate the depth for the seam allowance at each stage of your project.*
Topstitch. *With your work right side up, sew through all layers close to the edge or seam as indicated. To keep an even distance you can usually align the edge of your presser foot with the edge of your fabric or with the seam.*
Folded allowance. *A margin of fabric that is pressed to the wrong side along the edge of your work.*
Press the seam allowances open. *Lay your work seam-allowance side up on your ironing board; use the iron to separate the allowances so each lies flush against the work.*
Press the seam allowances to one side. *Lay your work seam-allowance side up on your ironing board; use the iron to press both allowances against the work on one side of the seamline.*

the straight stitch on your machine, sewing parallel to the edge at the distance indicated in the directions; keep the work flat and smooth and, if you did not baste, remove the pins as you sew.

- To make sure your seams stay sewn while you attach adjacent pieces and when the bag is used, backstitch for a short distance at the beginning and end of each.
- After sewing, trim the excess seam allowance properly so there are no unsightly lumps when you turn your work right side out: Cutting close to the stitches, diagonally trim the allowance across a corner point (fig. 11), clip (cut across) the allowance on inside curves, and cut triangular notches along outside curves (fig. 12).
- Every time you fold the fabric to create a hem or turn under an edge, press the fold with your iron: the next steps will be faster and easier, and the results more professional.

Hand stitches

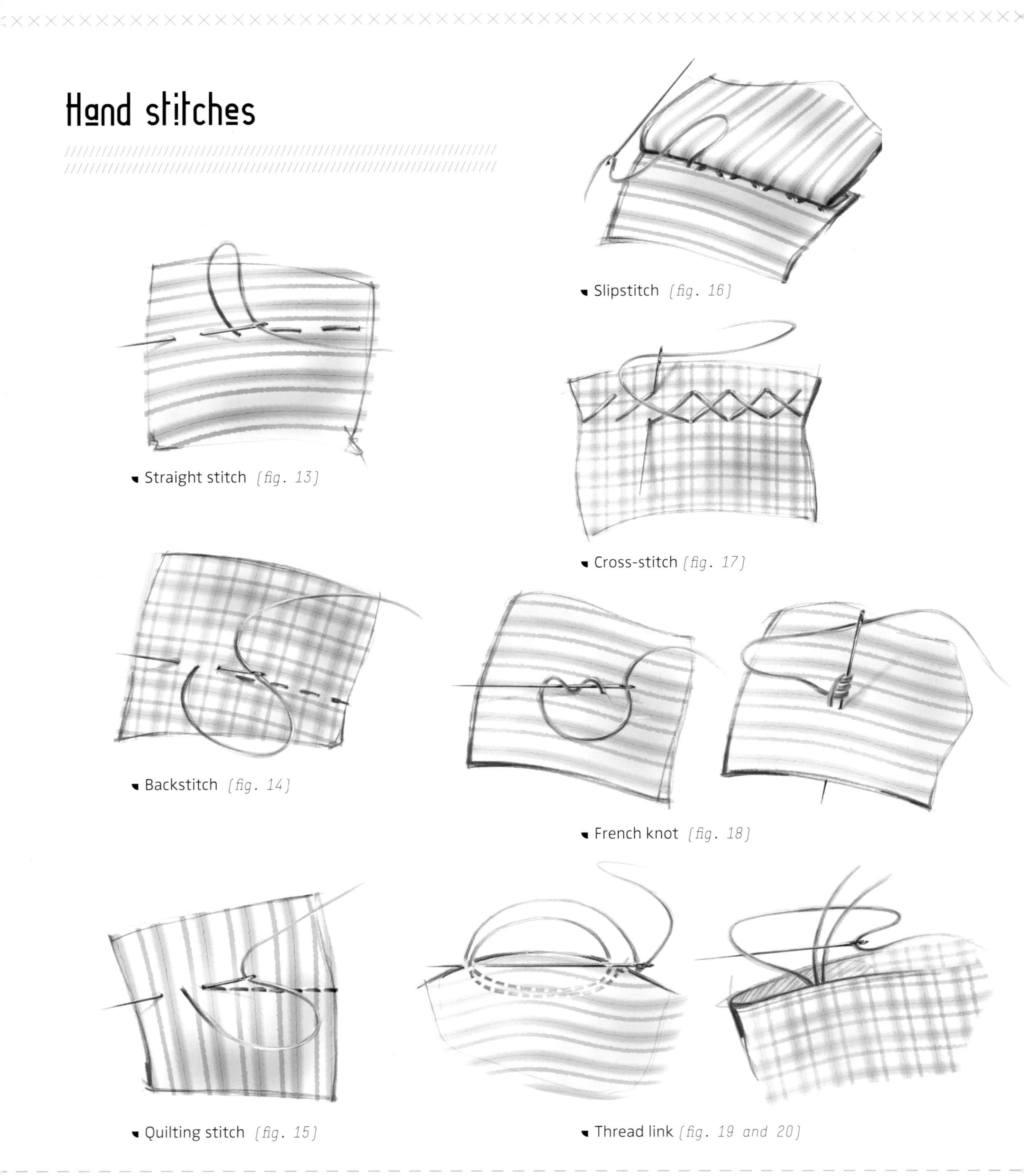

Straight stitch [fig. 13]

Backstitch [fig. 14]

Quilting stitch [fig. 15]

Slipstitch [fig. 16]

Cross-stitch [fig. 17]

French knot [fig. 18]

Thread link [fig. 19 and 20]

Note

In the text and drawings, the dimensions given for positioning snaps, buttons, etc. are always measured from the center of the snap or button.

Tips

- Coated, textured, and open-weave fabrics may not move smoothly through your sewing machine; they are prone to sticking or being caught in the presser foot or feed dogs. When this happens, there is a risk your fabric will be damaged. To prevent this, place the material between two pieces of tissue paper, align the edge of the paper with the edge of your work, and sew through all thicknesses. When the seam is done, gently tear off the paper. Alternatively, use a temporary interfacing specifically designed for this purpose.
- The lining may be lighter weight than the exterior of a bag. For best results, it should be just a little bit smaller too, so use a slightly deeper seam allowance than is indicated.
- If a bag is not lined, it's a good idea to topstitch the seam allowance to the main part of the fabric so the allowance stays flat. You can press the allowances open and topstitch each (fig. 21), or press them together to one side (fig. 22). In both cases, you might like to fold under the cut edge.
- When applying a patch pocket on the interior or exterior of your bag, reinforce the top corners by sewing a small triangle at each (fig. 23).
- The length to make the handles or straps is indicated for each bag. But you should feel free to adjust this to suit your taste or stature.
- Use heavy-duty thread instead of regular sewing thread to ensure the most durable seams. Or use a reinforcing utility stitch if your machine has one.
- If you are sewing together two different-color fabrics, always match the thread in the needle to the fabric that is on top while you sew, and use a bobbin that matches the fabric on the bottom. Don't be lazy—it's worth the bother to change the thread whenever needed.

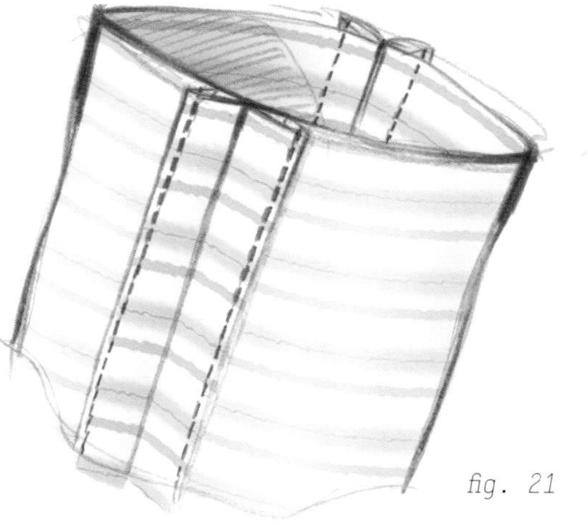

fig. 21

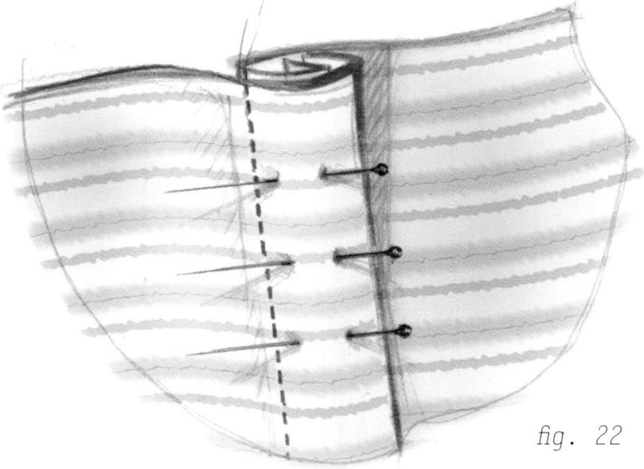

fig. 22

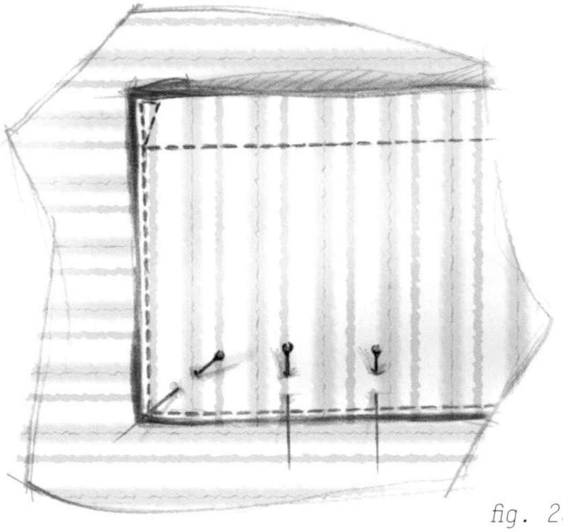

fig. 23

Prepare the pieces

Photocopy the three patterns on pages 138 and 139, enlarging the main piece to 155% and copying the closure flap and the gusset end detail in the size shown. *Turn to page 138 to see how to position the pieces on your fabric.*

Red felt - Mark and then cut 1 main piece.

Chocolate brown felt - Trace and then cut:

1 main piece;

1 gusset 3 1/8" x 40 1/2" (8 cm x 101,5 cm)

1 closure flap 3 1/8" x 6 3/4" (8 cm x 17 cm).

Cut both ends of the gusset using the detail pattern; then mark the shaded areas onto the side of the felt that will face the interior of your bag. Using the rotary cutter or small sharp scissors, cut the buttonholes in the closure flap as shown on the pattern, making each slightly larger than the diameter of your button.

1 With the wrong sides together, pin one long edge of the gusset to the red main piece, centering the gusset on the bottom (longer) edge of the main piece and aligning the top corners as shown. Baste; then, with doubled red thread, sew together about 1/4" (3 mm) from the edge, using a hand running stitch (see fig. 13, page 16).

Felt Kelly

Dimensions: 14 3/4" (37 cm) wide at base x 3 1/8" (8 cm) deep x 10 1/4" (26 cm) high (excluding the handle)

Tools

Sewing essentials (see page 7):
Fabric marker,
Cutting mat,
Ruler,
Rotary cutter,
Household scissors,
Leather needle,
Thimble,
2 clothespins.

Materials

- Red industrial felt, 1/4" (4-5 mm) thick: 14 3/4" x 10 1/4" (37 cm x 26 cm)
- Chocolate brown industrial felt, 1/4" (4-5 mm) thick: 13 3/8" x 40 1/2" (34 cm x 101.5 cm)
- Dark brown leather handle, fitted at each end with a metal ring 1 1/4" (3 cm) in diameter
- 2 red mother-of-pearl buttons, 1 1/4" (3 cm) in diameter
- Thread: red, chocolate brown
- Contact cement or strong glue

Be sure you have access to a photocopier for enlarging the pattern.

2 In the same manner as in step 1, pin the opposite long edge of the gusset to the brown felt main piece, and sew together using brown thread.

3 Slide each end of the gusset into a ring at the end of the handle (don't twist the handle). Apply glue to the marked areas on the gusset, allow to dry for 1 hour, apply glue again and let dry 20 minutes. Fold the gusset ends over the rings, press the glued areas together and secure with clothespins until completely dry.

4 Sew a button to each side of the bag, centered on and about 1¾" (4.5 cm) below the top edge. Button the closure flap over the top of the bag.

Tip

The closure flap will be easier to use if the buttons are not tight against the bag. To allow space for the felt flap to fit under the buttons, place a cocktail pick or a wooden match under each button while you sew it on (see fig. 1, page 10).

Note

The measurements given for positioning the buttons indicate the center of each button.

Tools

Sewing essentials (see page 7),
Felt-tip marker with nonpermanent ink,
Household scissors,
Embroidery needle,
Safety pin.

Materials

- Light green cotton: 14" x 28" (35 cm x 70 cm)
- Purple cotton: 3½" x 59" (8 cm x 150 cm)
- Pink felt, ⅛" (2-3 mm) thick: 10" x 4" (25 cm x 10 cm)
- Purple felt, ⅛" (2-3 mm) thick: 8" x 4" (20 cm x 10 cm)
- Translucent, yellow, 4-hole buttons: five ⅝" (1.5 cm) in diameter; two ¾" in diameter
- Thread: light green, purple
- Yellow embroidery floss

Little flowers

Dimensions: 13" (34 cm) wide x 12¾" (30 cm) high

Prepare the pieces

Trace the five flower patterns on page 140.

Light green cotton - Mark and then cut 1 main piece the size indicated in the materials list.

Purple cotton - Mark and then cut 2 drawstrings 1¾" x 59" (4 cm x 150 cm).

Serge or zigzag the edges of each piece of fabric.

Felt - Using the patterns, cut: 1 flower A, 2 flowers B, and 1 flower C from pink felt; 1 flower C, 1 flower D, and 1 flower E from purple felt.

Cut slashes all around flower E as shown on the pattern.

1 Fold the main piece in half, right side in, bringing the shorter edges together. Starting at the fold (bottom of bag) pin the layers together along each side. Baste and then sew the side seams, using ½" (1 cm) seam allowance; begin stitching ¾" (2 cm) from the bottom fold and stop 2" (5 cm) from the top edge.

2 Press the seam allowances open, fold back and press the allowances at the open top of each seam. Sew along each opening close to the edge of the fold, pivoting across the seam.

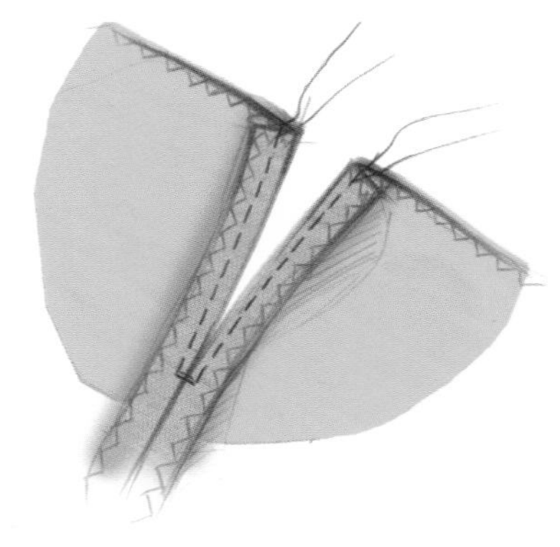

3 To make a casing for the drawstring at the top of each section, fold and press ¼" (5 mm) to the wrong side, then fold and press 1" (2.5 cm) to the wrong side. Stitch each casing close to the first fold. Turn the bag right side out.

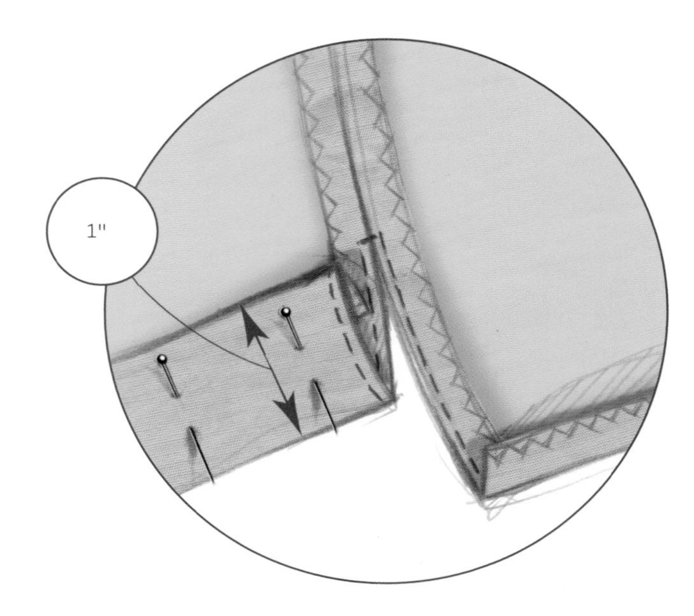

4 Fold and press 1/4" (5 mm) to the wrong side on the long edges of each drawstring. Then, with the right side out, fold each in half lengthwise; press. Sew each drawstring through all layers, close to each fold.

5 Using the safety pin as a guide and beginning and ending at the same side seam, thread one drawstring through both casings; adjust it so the extending tails are equal. Beginning and ending at the other side seam, repeat with the second drawstring.

6 At one side of the bag, hold the ends of drawstring together. Insert them through the opening in the side seam at the bottom of the bag. Repeat with the other drawstring and the other side seam. Turn the bag wrong side out.

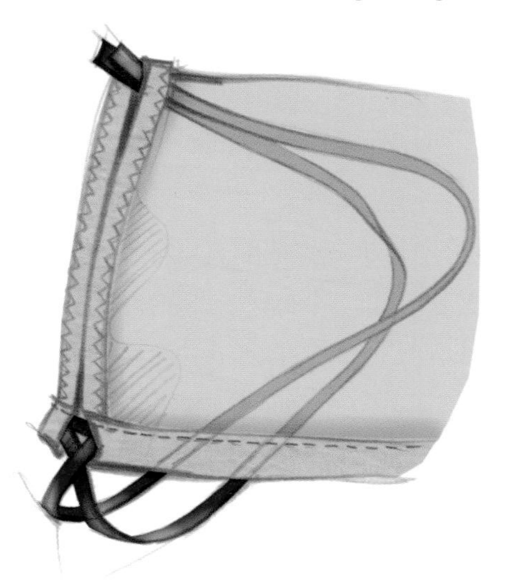

Unfold the seam allowances and finish sewing each side seam through all layers, securing the drawstring ends. Turn the bag right side out.

7 Pin the felt flowers to the outside of the bag as shown in the drawings and photos.

Place a button in the center of each flower and sew it to the bag using embroidery floss, stitching diagonally through the holes to form an X in the middle of each button (see fig. 17, page 16); use the larger buttons on the two C flowers.

Tip

When threading the drawstring through the casing, push against the safety pin, gathering and then smoothing the casing fabric with your fingers until the pin emerges at the opposite end.

Prepare the pieces

Turn to page 141 to see how to position the pieces on your fabrics.

Linen - Mark and then cut:
2 main pieces 12½" x 11" (32 cm x 28 cm);
1 gusset 4" x 32" (11 cm x 82 cm);
2 handles 1½" x 14½" (4 cm x 37 cm);
1 snap hook strap 1½" x 9" (4 cm x 23 cm).

Striped cotton - With the stripes oriented as shown on page 141, mark and then cut:
6 pieces identical to those cut in linen;
1 interior pocket 8" x 6¼" (20 cm x 16 cm).
Serge or zigzag the edges of each piece.

Batting - Mark and then cut:
2 main pieces 11½" x 9½" (30 cm x 25 cm);
1 gusset 3" x 30½" (9 cm x 80 cm).

1 To assemble the exterior of the bag (linen), with the wrong sides together, pin one long edge of the gusset to each main piece, centering the gusset on the bottom (longer) edge of the main pieces and aligning the top corners. Sew together using ½" (1 cm) seam allowance. Trim the seam allowance at the lower corners. Along the top edge, press ½" (1 cm) to the wrong side. Turn the bag right side out.

Suspender satchel

Dimensions: 11½" (30 cm) wide x 3" (9 cm) deep x 10" (26 cm) high (excluding the handles)

Tools

Sewing essentials (see page 7),
Felt-tip marker with nonpermanent ink,
Leather needle,
Thimble.

Materials

- Natural color linen: 18" x 32" (47 cm x 82 cm)
- Striped cotton (stripes parallel long edge): 18" x 32" (47 cm x 82 cm)
- Lightweight batting: 14" x 30½" (35 cm x 80 cm)
- 3 sets of button-on suspender fasteners, approximately 3½" (9 cm) long: 2 fitted with a ¾" (2 cm) wide oval ring; 1 secured in a leather medallion (see photos)
- 6 gray mother-of-pearl buttons, sized to fit the suspender fittings
- 1 snap hook
- Ecru thread
- Spray adhesive for fabric

2 Repeat step 1 using the corresponding striped cotton pieces to make the lining.

3 On one long edge of the interior pocket, fold and press 1/4" (1 cm) and then 1/2" (2 cm) to the wrong side. Pin; then sew through all layers close to the first fold. On the other long edge and then on each side, fold and press 1/4" (1 cm) to the wrong side.

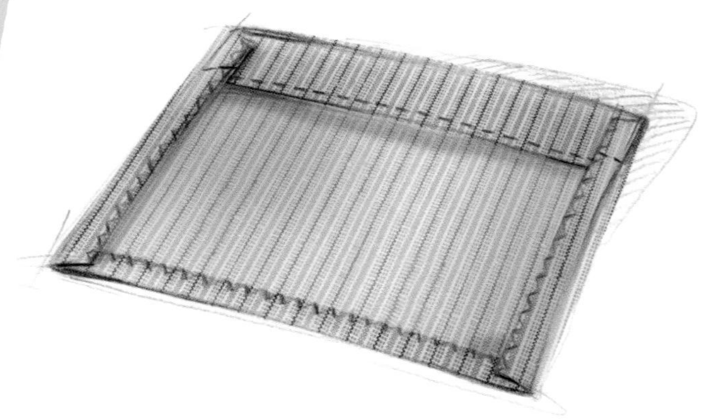

4 Pin the pocket to the middle of one of the main pieces of the lining, placing the wrong side of the pocket against the right side of the lining. Sew the pocket to the lining, stitching close to the side and bottom edges and reinforcing the top corners with a small triangle (see fig. 23, page 17). Divide the pocket into two compartments by stitching from top to bottom parallel to the sides.

5 On the long edges of all the handles, fold and press 1/4" (1 cm) to the wrong side. With the wrong sides together and long edges aligned, pin each linen handle to a striped cotton handle. Sew each pair together close to the edges.

6 Mist one side of each piece of batting with adhesive and then, aligning its top edge below the pressed under seam allowance, affix it to the wrong side of the corresponding section of the linen bag. Press the bag between your hands to adhere the layers. With the striped side facing toward the outside of the bag, curve one of the handles above the top edge of one main piece; align the ends of the handle with the edge of the top seam allowance and place each one about 2 1/2" (6 cm) from a side seam. Pin securely. Make sure the linen bag is right side out. Turn the lining wrong side out and insert it in the bag, aligning the seams. Pin together along the top edge. Sew through all layers, close to the edge and again 3/8" (1 cm) below the edge.

7 Sew buttons to the outside of the bag on the side opposite the handle, aligning them 1 1/2" (4 cm) below the top edge and placing them in pairs 1 3/4" (4.5 cm) and 3 3/4" (8.5 cm) from each side seam as shown. Using the leather needle

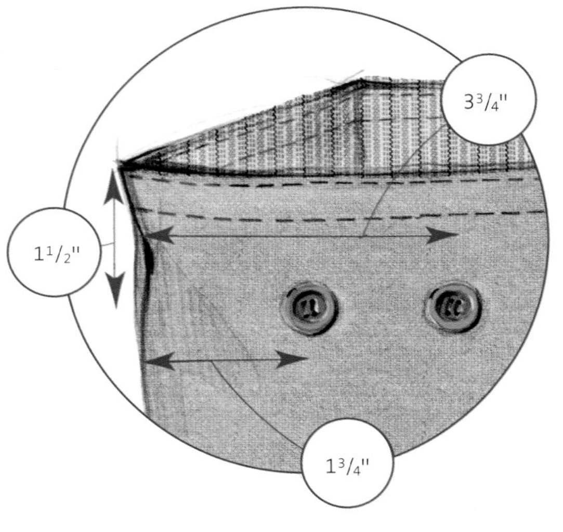

and referring to the drawing below, sew the suspender fastener with the leather medallion to the bag between the button pairs.

8 Sew two buttons to the outside of the bag on the side with the handle, placing each about 5" (13 cm) from a side seam; fold the suspender attachment over the open bag to determine the how far down to sew the buttons.

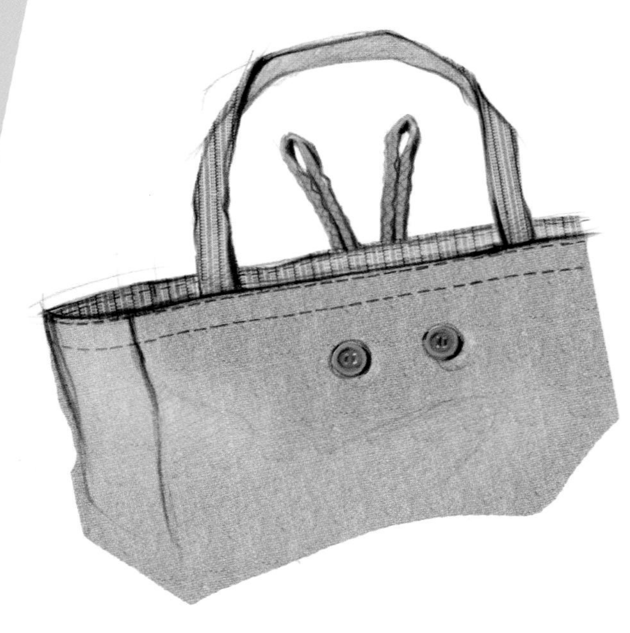

9 Button the remaining suspender fasteners onto the bag. With the striped side facing out, fold the ends of the remaining strap through the fasteners as shown. Adjust the strap length to equal the first strap. Allowing enough fabric to fold under the raw ends, cut off the excess. Sew each end to itself, enclosing the metal bar.

10 Follow step 5 to construct the snap hook strap. With the linen side out, insert one end of the strap through the ring of the snap hook; fold under the raw end and sew the end to itself securely, enclosing the metal bar. Fold under the other end of the strap, folding the striped fabric against itself. Insert the strap into the bag, with the striped side facing the gusset lining and the folded end facing up; sew the folded end to the gusset below the top edge.

The suspender fasteners will be easier to use if the buttons are not tight against the bag. To allow space for the fasteners to fit under the buttons, place a cocktail pick or a wooden match under each button while you sew it on (see fig. 1, page 10).

Note

The measurements given for positioning the buttons indicate the center of each button.

Tools

Sewing essentials (see page 7), Felt-tip marker with nonpermanent ink.

Materials

For the «daytime» side

- Pink taffeta: $10\frac{1}{2}$" x 40" (27,5 cm x 100 cm)
- Pink/chartreuse chenille ribbon, $\frac{3}{8}$" (1 cm) wide: 36" (96 cm)
- Pink/chartreuse chenille ribbon, $\frac{3}{4}$" (1.8 cm) wide: 36" (96 cm)

For the «evening» side

- Purple taffeta: $10\frac{1}{2}$" x 40" (27.5 cm x 100 cm)
- Light pink velvet ribbon, $\frac{1}{4}$" (5 mm) wide: 36" (96 cm)
- Periwinkle velvet ribbon, $\frac{3}{8}$" (1 cm) wide: 18" (48 cm)
- Purple velvet ribbon, $\frac{3}{8}$" (1 cm) wide: 36" (96 cm)
- Pink velvet ribbon, $\frac{5}{8}$" (1.5 cm) wide: 18" (48 cm)
- Pink satin ribbon, $\frac{3}{8}$" (1 cm) wide: 36" (96 cm)
- Fuchsia bead-trimmed organza ribbon, $\frac{3}{4}$" (2 cm) wide: 36" (96 cm)
- Purple, beaded picot-edge crochet trim, $\frac{3}{8}$" (7 mm) wide: 18" (48 cm)

For both sides

- Thread: pink, purple

Reversible charmer

Dimensions: 8" (22 cm) wide x 9" (28 cm) high (excluding the strap)

Prepare the pieces

Taffetas - For each color, mark and then cut:
1 main piece 9" x 23" (24 cm x 58 cm);
1 strap $1\frac{1}{2}$" x 40" (3.5 cm x 100 cm).
Serge or zigzag the edges of all pieces.
Ribbons - Cut each ribbon into 9" (24 cm) lengths.

1 Following the drawings below and measuring from one end of each piece of taffeta, arrange the ribbons as shown. Baste them in place. Measuring from the other end of each piece of taffeta, repeat the arrangement in reverse and baste the ribbons in place.

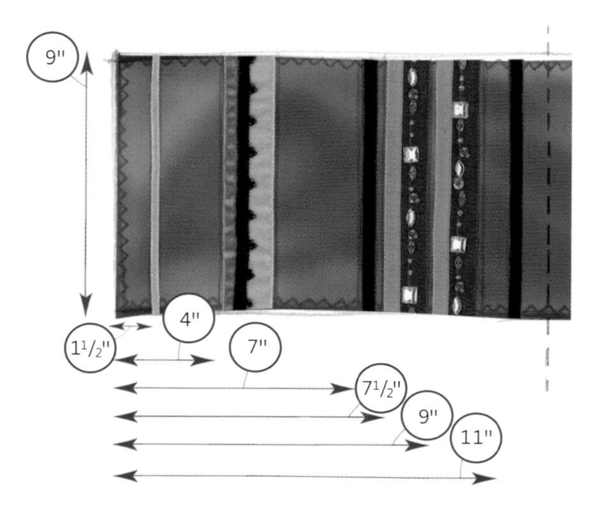

2 Sew on the ribbons as follows: for the ribbons on the pink taffeta and for all the velvet ribbons, sew close to both edges of each ribbon; to allow them to hang well, sew the other ribbons only along their top edge (the middle of the fabric will be the bottom of the bag).

3 Fold each ribbon-trimmed piece of taffeta in half, ribbon-side in, bringing the shorter edges together. Make sure the ribbon ends match along the sides. Pin and baste the layers together along the sides; then sew, using ½" (1 cm) seam allowance. At the end of each seam next to the fold, trim the seam allowance at an angle. Turn each bag right side out.

4 At the top of each bag, fold and then press ½" (1 cm) to the inside.

5 On the long edges of both straps, fold and press ¼" (5 mm) to the wrong side. With the wrong sides together and long edges aligned, pin the straps together. Sew together close to the edges.

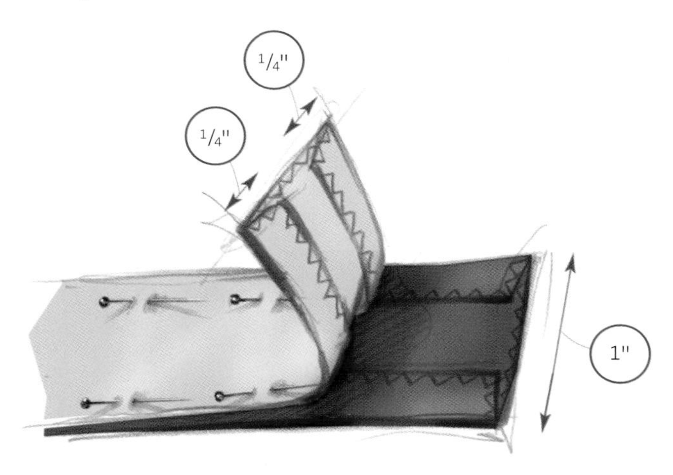

6 Make sure the purple bag is right side out. Turn the pink bag inside out and insert it in the purple bag; align the side seams and top edges and pin the bags together along the top. Insert the ends of the strap between the bags at the top of each side seam; make sure the purple side faces out and pin the strap in place. Referring to the drawing at right, insert the end of a piece of light pink velvet ribbon between the bags at the top center of each side; pin. Baste and then sew the bags together close to the top edge.

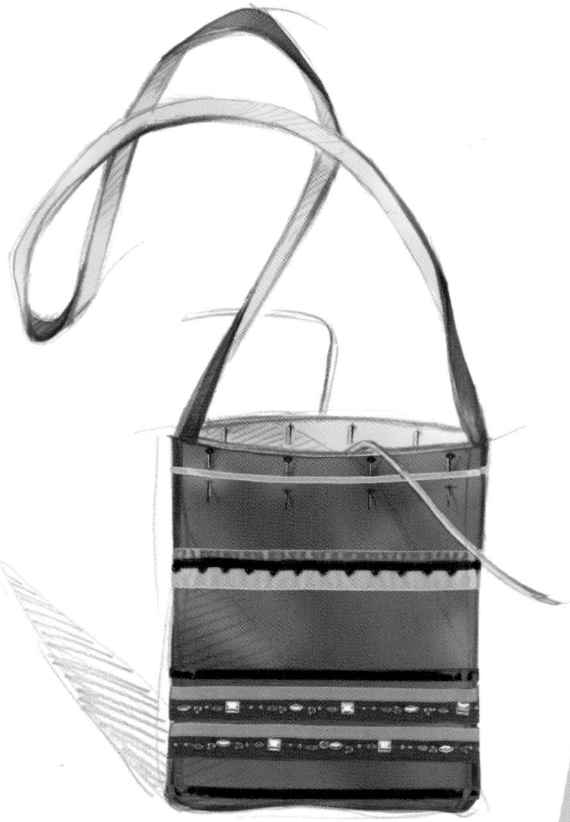

Prepare the pieces

Cut both fabrics to the size indicated in the materials list; make sure the stripes parallel the long edge. Serge or zigzag the edges of both pieces.

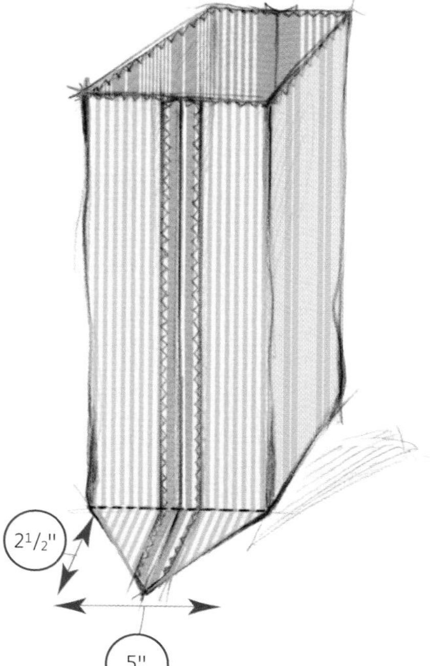

1 Fold the striped fabric in half, right side in, bringing the shorter edges together. Pin the layers together along the sides; then sew, using ½" (1 cm) seam allowance. Press the seam allowances open, trimming them at an angle next to the fold. Fold and press ½" (1 cm) to the wrong side along the top (open end) of the bag.

2 To box each bottom corner of the bag, align the side seam on the bottom fold, forming a triangle measuring 5" (12 cm) at the base. Sew through all layers at the base of each triangle and fold the triangles onto the bottom of the bag.

3 Repeat steps 1 and 2 with the herringbone fabric to make the lining.

To the beach

Dimensions: 9" (23 cm) wide x 5" (12 cm) deep x 14½" (37 cm) high (excluding the handles)

Tools

Sewing essentials (see page 7),
Felt-tip marker with nonpermanent ink.

Materials

- Off-white/taupe striped mattress ticking: 15" x 35" (37 cm x 88 cm)
- Off-white/taupe herringbone mattress ticking(for the lining): 15" x 35" (37 cm x 88 cm)
- Off-white webbing (for the straps), 1½" (4 cm) wide: 2¾ yards (226 cm)
- 2 off-white pom-poms with flat backs, on tie-tack fittings or snaps
- Off-white thread

4 Using $^{1}/_{2}$" (1 cm) seam allowance, sew the ends of the webbing together to form a ring (make sure the webbing isn't twisted). Press the seam allowances open.

5 Turn the striped bag right side out. Following the drawing below, pin the strap to it: place the strap seam on the bottom, allowing $1^{1}/_{4}$" (3 cm) between each corner and the stap and letting the strap form handles at the top.

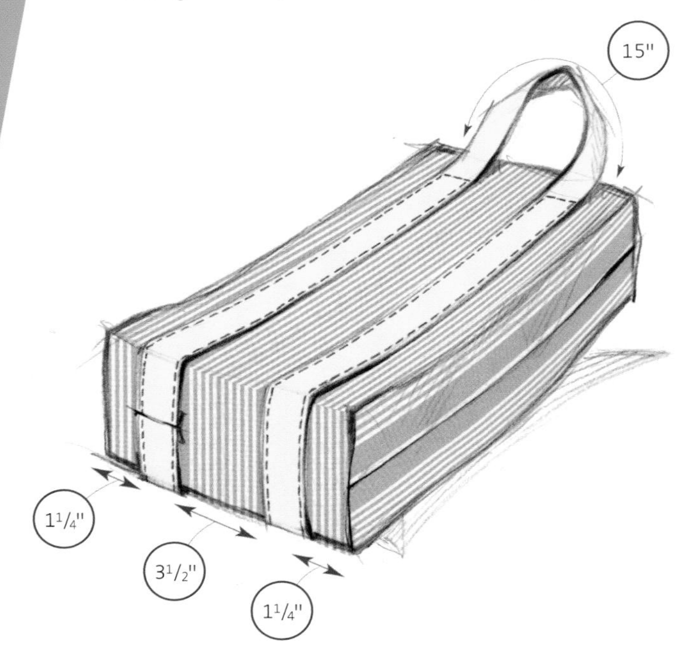

Baste the strap to the bag. Sew it on, stitching close to both long edges and pivoting across it about $1^{1}/_{2}$" (4 cm) below the top of the bag.

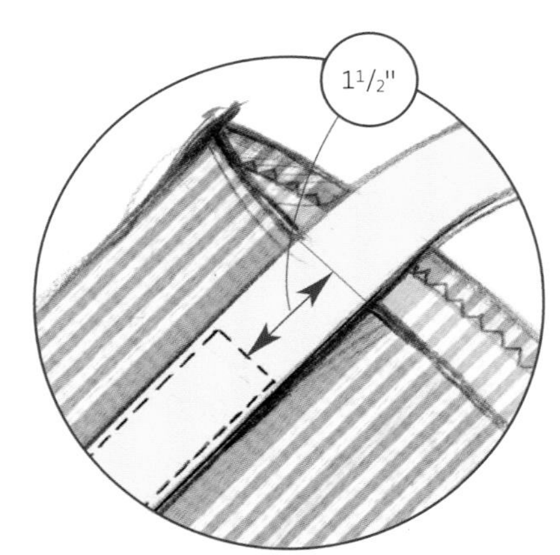

6 Make sure the striped bag is right side out and the lining wrong side out. Insert the lining in the bag, aligning the side seams and top edges. Pin and then baste together along the top edge. Sew together, stitching close to the top edge; be sure to keep the handles free.

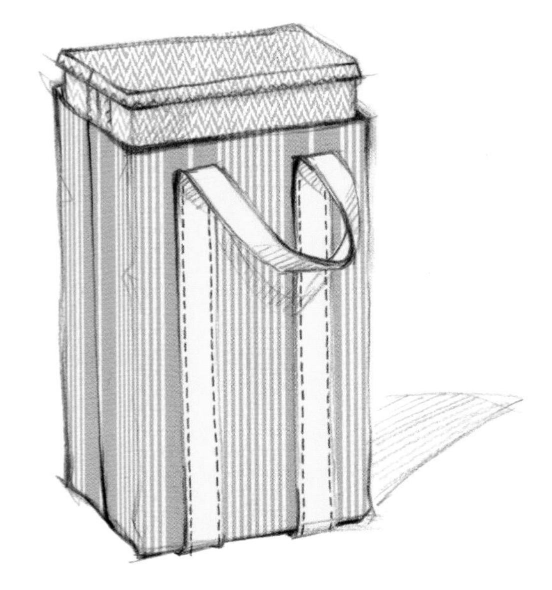

7 To make handgrips, fold the webbing in each handle in half lengthwise; pin and then baste the open edges of each closed. Sew close to the edge, starting and stopping about $2^{1}/_{2}$" (6 cm) from the stitches securing the strap to the bag.

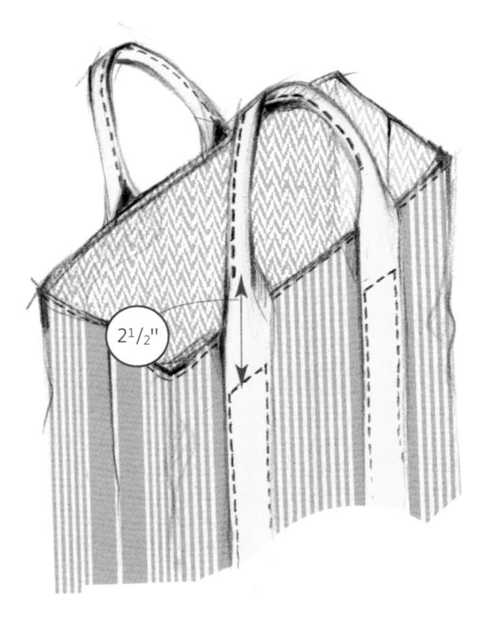

8 Pin a pom-pom to each strap as shown in the photos; if you don't have tie-tack fastenings, affix the pom-poms to the bag with snaps or simply sew them on.

Tip

For sturdy results, use heavy-duty thread instead of regular sewing thread to attach the webbing straps to the bag–they'll hold more weight and resist coming loose.

Tools

Sewing essentials (see page 7),
Ballpoint pen,
Pencil,
Household scissors,
Cutting mat,
Ruler,
Rotary cutter,
Grommet-setting tools.

Materials

- Vinyl-coated print fabric for the exterior: 31" x 32" (76 cm x 85 cm)
- Vinyl-coated print fabric for the lining: 28" x 32" (69 cm x 85 cm)
- Lightweight batting: 4" x 15" (10 cm x 38 cm)
- Medium-weight cardboard (for stiffener) 1/8" (3 mm) thick: 7" x 19" (19 cm x 48 cm)
- Webbing (to support the grommets) 1 1/2" (4 cm) wide: 8" (20 cm)
- 4 grommets 3/4" (2 cm) in diameter
- Thread to match fabric

Country print tote

Dimensions: 19" (48 cm) wide x 7" (17 cm) deep x 12" (31 cm) tall (excluding the handles)

Prepare the pieces

Turn to page 141 to see how to position the pieces on your fabrics.

Exterior cloth - Mark and then cut:
1 main piece 20" x 32" (50 cm x 85 cm);
2 gussets 8" x 13" (19 cm x 33 cm);
2 handles 3" x 16" (7 cm x 40 cm).

Lining - Mark and then cut:
1 main piece 20" x 32" (50 cm x 85 cm);
2 gussets 8" x 13" (19 cm x 33 cm).

On the wrong side of the fabric, mark the midpoint of both long edges of each main piece and the midpoint of one end of each gusset.

Batting - Mark and then cut 2 pieces 2" x 15" (5 cm x 38 cm).

Cardboard - Mark and then cut 1 piece the size indicated in the materials list.

Webbing - Cut into 4 pieces of equal length.

1 Arrange the main piece and gussets for the exterior of the bag as shown in the drawing below. One at a time, turn each gusset right side down on the main piece; align the marks and pin the end of each to the main piece. Using 1/2" (1 cm) seam allowance and beginning and ending 1/2" (1 cm) from the long edges of the gussets, sew each gusset to the main piece.

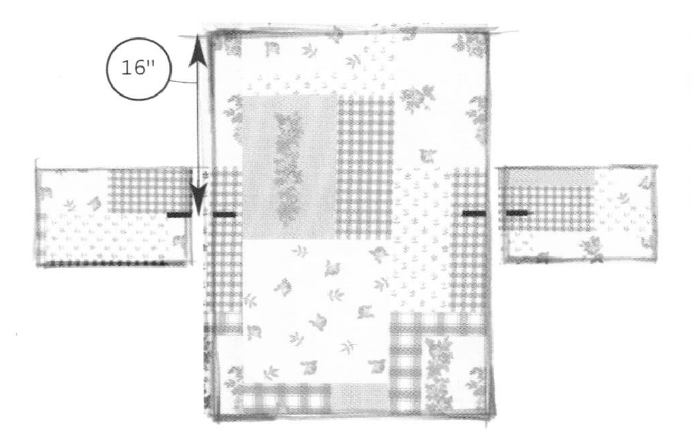

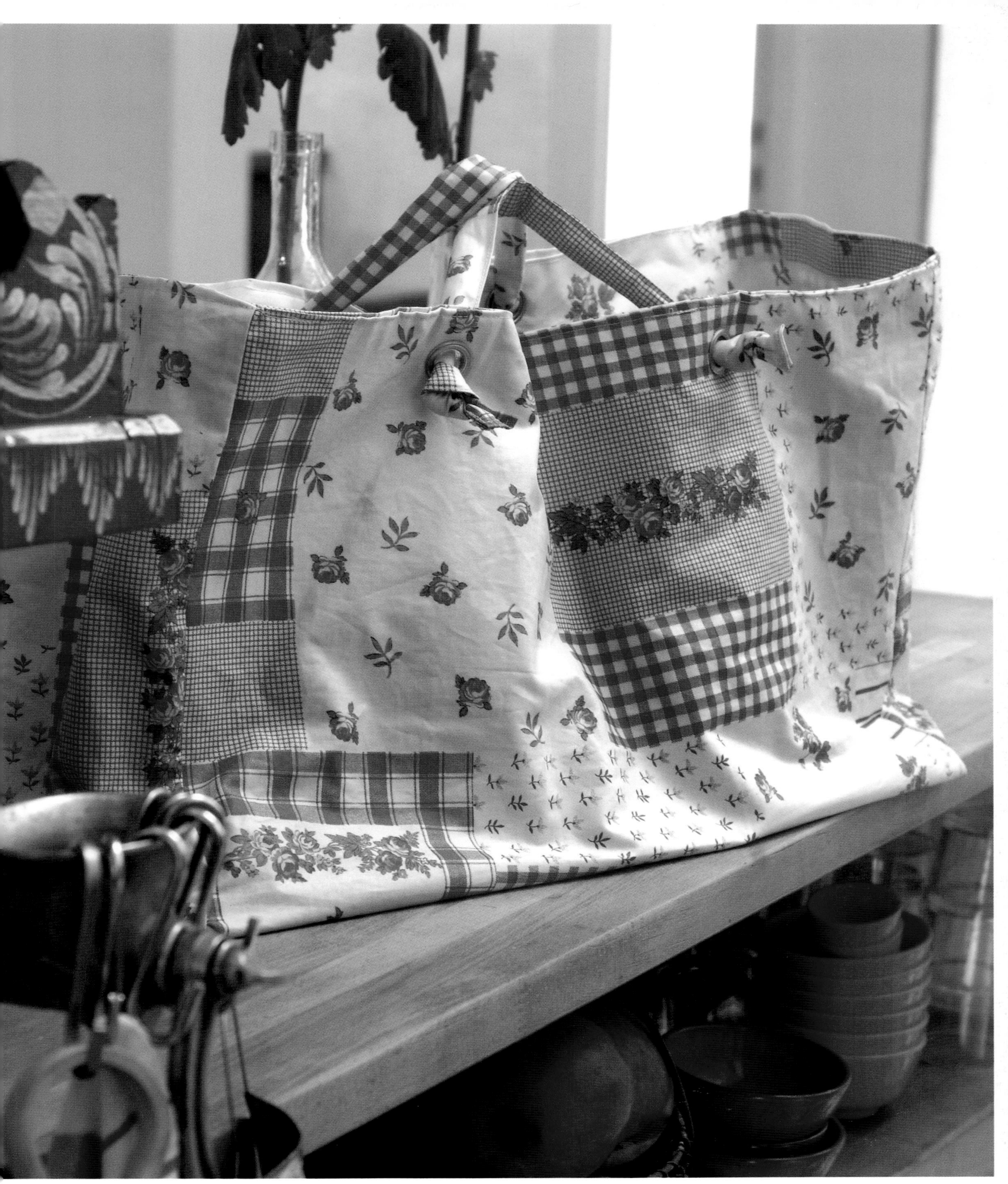

2 Pin the long edges of each gusset to the adjacent side edge of the main piece; sew, using ½" (1 cm) seam allowance. Trim the seam allowance at the lower corners. Along the top edge, press ½" (1 cm) to the wrong side.

3 Repeat steps 1 and 2 to sew the lining gussets to the lining main piece.

4 Turn the exterior bag right side out. Place the cardboard in the bottom. Make sure the lining is wrong side out and insert it in the exterior bag, aligning the seams. On the top edges of the main lining piece, measure 4" (11 cm) from each gusset and slip a piece of webbing under the turned down top allowance; pin so the pin heads extend above the top. Pin the top edges of the exterior and lining together and sew through all layers close to the edge.

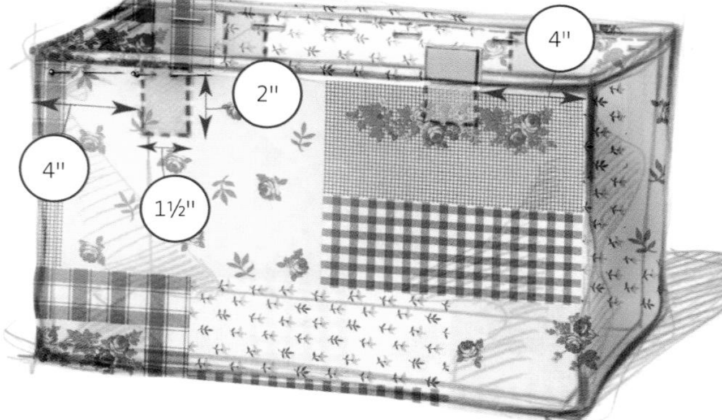

5 Center a piece of batting on the wrong side of each handle. Fold the margin of cloth over the batting on all edges; baste. Fold each handle in half lengthwise, batting side in; pin the layers together along the three open edges. Sew each handle through all layers, close to the edges.

6 Placing them where each piece of webbing is located and 1¼" (3 cm) below the top edge, apply the grommets (see page 12). Place one handle inside the bag, pass the ends through the grommets on one main section; knot on the outside of the bag. Repeat with the remaining handle on the other main section of the bag.

Tips

Coated fabric is tricky to work with, especially if it is coated with a vinyl waterproofing substance. Holes from misplaced stitches may show unattractively, so measure carefully and test your assembly using tape instead of pins so you can adjust the seamlines if needed. Be sure to clip the main pieces where they turn to form the lower corners of the bag.

Pin the pieces together in the seam allowances so the holes will not show on your finished bag. When putting two folded edges together (as at the top of the bag), either pin exactly on the seamline, or use a fabric adhesive to hold the layers in position.

To help the coated fabric move smoothly through the sewing machine, and to keep the feed dogs from marring the coated surface, place your work between two pieces of tissue paper or an interfacing specifically formulated to facilitate this kind of work. When you've finished the seam, tear off the tissue or interfacing.

Note

The measurement given for positioning the grommets indicates the center of each grommet.

Prepare the pieces

Turn to page 143 to see how to position the pieces on your fabric.

Toile de Jouy -Mark and then cut:

2 main pieces 16" x 13½" (40 cm x 34 cm);

1 interior pocket 8½" x 6½" (21 cm x 16 cm).

Chambray - Mark and then cut 2 main pieces 16" x 13½" (40 cm x 34 cm).

Serge or zigzag the perimeter of each piece.

1 Lay the main pieces of toile right sides together. Pin the layers together along the bottom (wider) edge and both sides. Sew, using ½" (1 cm) seam allowance, beginning and ending 3½" (7.5 cm) from the top (open) edge.

3½"

13½"

16"

Loves me, loves me not

Dimensions: 15" (38 cm) wide at the base x 11" (28,5 cm) high (excluding the handles)

Tools

Sewing essentials (see page 7), Felt-tip pen with nonpermanent ink.

Materials

- Blue-and-ecru toile de Jouy: 32" x 20" (80 cm x 50 cm)
- Blue chambray (for the lining): 32" x 13½" (80 cm x 34 cm)
- 2 tassels with passementerie medallions
- 1 pair circular rattan handles, approximately 7" (18 cm) in diameter
- Thread: ecru, blue

2 Trim the seam allowance at the bottom corners diagonally. Press the seam allowances open, fold back and press the allowances at the open top of each seam. Sew along each opening close to the edge of the fold,

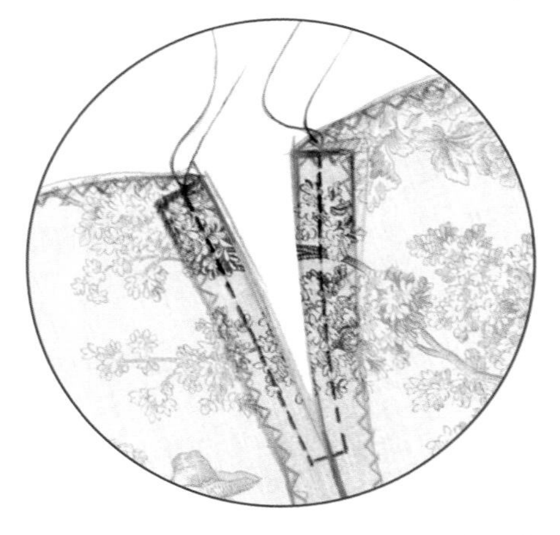

pivoting across the seam. At the top of each piece, fold and press ½" (1 cm) to the wrong side. Turn the bag right side out.

3 Repeat steps 1 and 2 using the chambray pieces to make the lining.

4 On the top (longer) edge of the interior pocket, fold and press ¼" (1 cm) and then ½" (2 cm) to the wrong side. Pin; then sew through all layers close to the first fold. On the other long edge and then on each side, fold and press ¼" (5 mm) to the wrong side.

5 Pin the pocket to one of the lining pieces, placing the wrong side of the pocket against the right side of the lining and centering it about 1¼" (3 cm) above the bottom seam. Sew the pocket to the lining, stitching close to the side and bottom edges and reinforcing the top corners with a small triangle (see fig. 23, page 17).

6 Make sure the lining is wrong side out. Insert it in the toile bag, aligning the seams and the top edges. Pin the top edges of each section together and also the open edges at the top of each side seam. Sew close to the edge through all layers, pivoting at each corner and side seam.

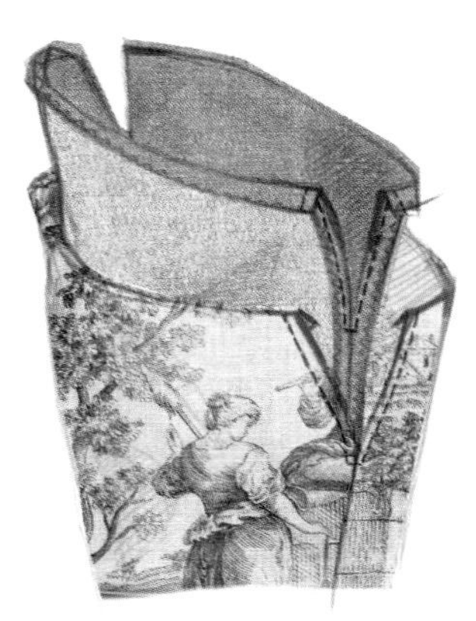

7 Fold the top of each section of the bag to the inside, enclosing one of the handles; pin as shown in the drawing below. Baste and then sew through all layers (use a zipper foot if needed). To finish, sew a tassel to each bottom corner of the bag, stitching neatly by hand through all layers.

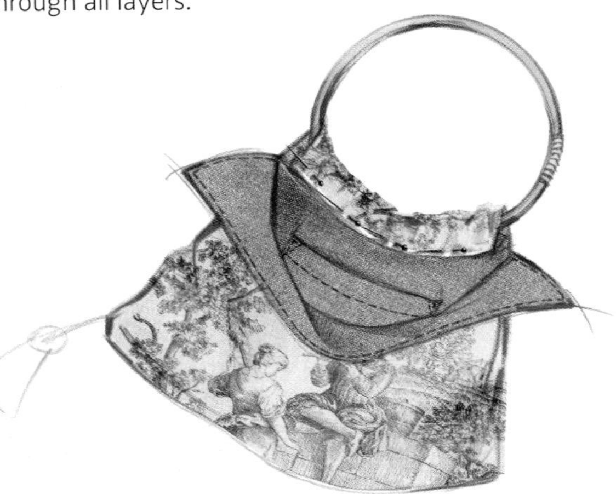

LES NOUVEA
RONSARD

Tools

Sewing essentials (see page 7),
Felt-tip pen with nonpermanent ink.

Materials

- Natural-color burlap: 46" x 44" (114 cm x 106 cm)
- Orange cotton canvas: 46" x 26½" (114 cm x 63 cm)
- 4 wood buttons, 1¼" (3.5 cm) in diameter
- Thread: orange, burlap-color

Smart carryall

Dimensions: 14" (35 cm) wide x 8" (20 cm) deep x 17" (41 cm) high (excluding the handles)

Prepare the pieces

Turn to page 142 to see how to position the pieces on your fabric.

Burlap - Mark and then cut:
4 main pieces 23" x 17½" (57 cm x 42 cm);
1 bottom 14" x 8" (37 cm x 22 cm).

Canvas - Mark and then cut: 2 lower borders 23" x 5" (57 cm x 11 cm); 1 bottom 14" x 8" (37 cm x 22 cm); 1 inside pocket 9" x 8" (21 cm x 19 cm); 2 binding strips 23" x 2½" (57 cm x 6 cm); 2 short handles 5" x 20" (12 cm x 47 cm); 2 long handles 5" x 29" (12 cm x 73 cm).

Serge the edges of each piece. Mark the midpoint on the ends of each bottom.

1 On the wrong side of the fabric, mark the seamline ½" (1 cm) from one long edge of each canvas border. With the right sides together, place each border on a burlap main piece, positioning the seamline 4½" (10 cm) from the lower (longer) edge of each as shown below. Pin and then sew each border to its burlap, stitching on the marked line. Fold the borders down, aligning their edges with the burlap edges. Press; then baste around the edges. Topstitch each border close to the fold through all thicknesses.

4"

4½"

2 Place the two main pieces just assembled right sides together, aligning the borders. Pin the side seams, then sew each using $1/2$" (1 cm) seam allowance. Press the seam allowances open.

3 With the right sides together, pin the canvas bottom into the assembled burlap/canvas main pieces, aligning the mark at each end of the bottom with a side seam. Baste; then sew, using $1/2$" (1 cm) seam allowance. At the corners, clip the burlap seam allowance and notch the canvas seam allowance. Press the allowances open. Turn the bag right side out.

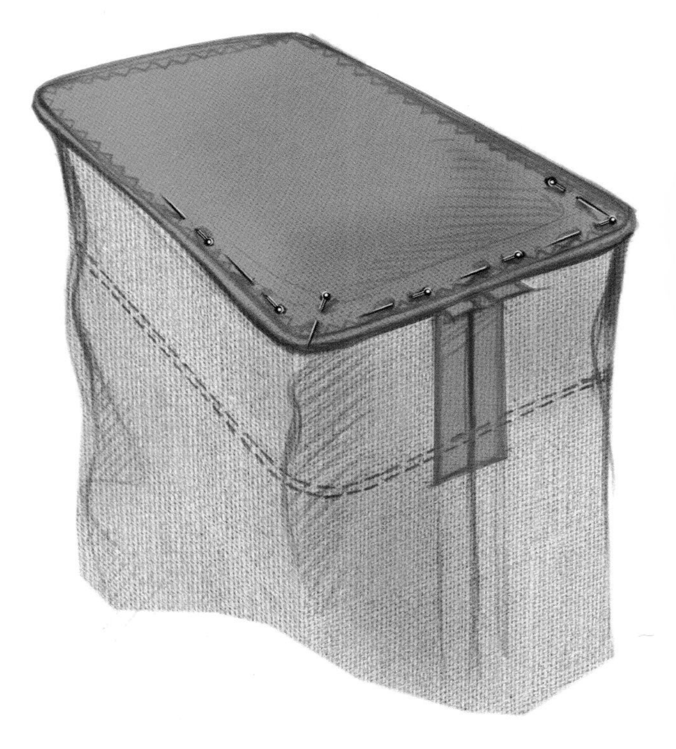

4 Disregarding the references to the canvas, follow steps 2 and 3 to assemble the lining from the remaining burlap pieces. Be sure to join the shorter edges of the burlap main pieces for the side seams.

5 On the top (longer) edge of the interior pocket, fold and press ¼" (1 cm) and then ½" (3 cm) to the wrong side. Pin; then sew through all layers close to the first fold. On the other long edge and then on each side, fold and press ¼" (1 cm) to the wrong side. Pin the pocket to one lining piece, placing the wrong side of the pocket against the right side of the lining and centering it about 4" (10 cm) below the top. Sew the pocket to the lining, stitching close to the side and bottom edges and reinforcing the top corners with a small triangle (see fig. 23, page 17).

6 Make sure the canvas-trimmed bag is right side out and the lining wrong side out. Insert the lining in the canvas-trimmed bag, aligning the seams and top edges. Pin and then baste the layers together along the top edge.

7 With the right sides together and using ½" (1 cm) seam allowance, sew the ends of the binding strips together to form a ring. Fold and press ¼" (1 cm) to the wrong side on each edge of the ring. Pin the ring, right side out, around the top of the bag, aligning the seams and leaving half the ring extending above the top. Topstitch the ring to bag, stitching close to the lower edge. Fold the ring over the top of the bag and slipstitch the edge to the inside (see fig. 16, page 16).

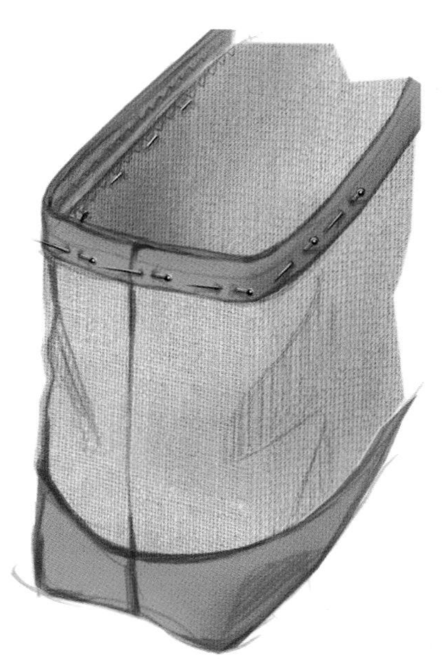

8 On all edges of each handle, fold and press ½" (1 cm) to the wrong side. Fold each handle in half lengthwise, wrong side in. Pin each handle closed along the open edges; then sew all around, through all layers, close to the edge.

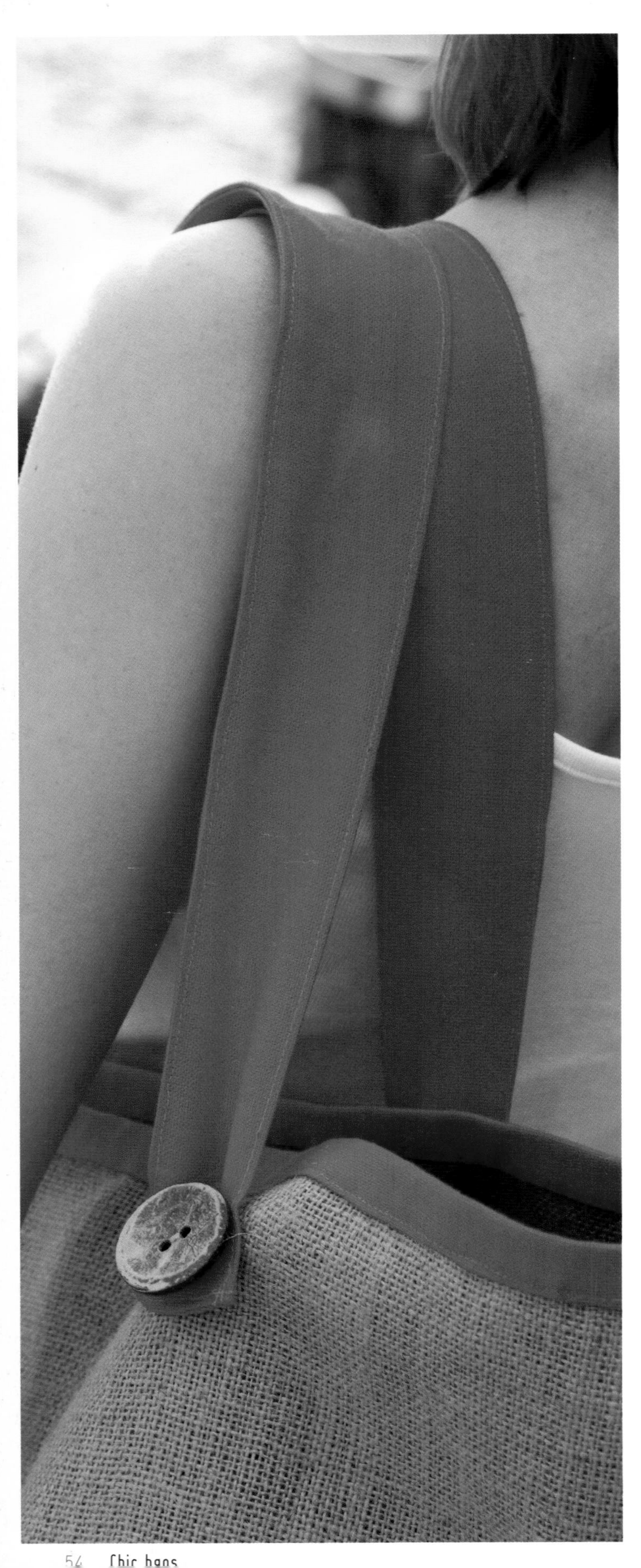

9 Referring to your sewing machine manual, mark and sew a $1\frac{3}{8}$" (3.5 cm) buttonhole (or the size to accommodate your button) at each end of each handle, placing it parallel to and $1\frac{1}{4}$" (3 cm) from the end of the handle. Cut each buttonhole open. On the long edges of each short

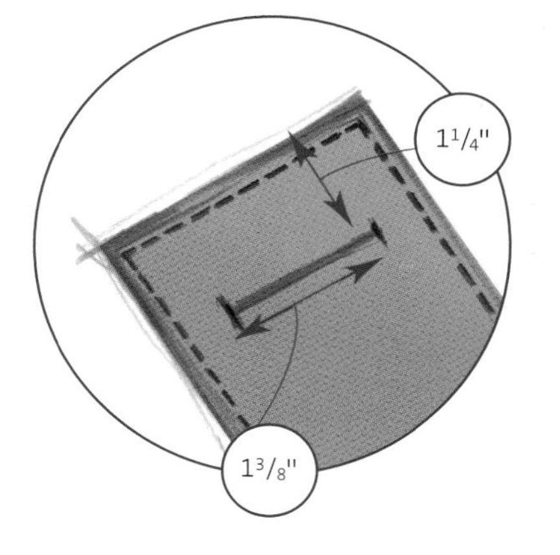

handle, mark the point $4\frac{1}{2}$" (15 cm) from each end. Fold each short handle in half lengthwise; pin and then topstitch its long edges together between the marks, stitching close to the edge. Sew the buttons to the outside of the bag, placing them 2" (5 cm) below the top edge and 7" (17 cm) from each side seam. Button on whichever pair of handles you prefer.

Tips

For sturdy results, use heavy-duty thread instead of regular sewing thread to assemble the bag—the seams will support more weight.

The handles will be easier to attach if the buttons are not tight against the bag. To allow space for the handle to fit under the buttons, place a cocktail pick or a wooden match under each button while you sew it on (see fig. 1, page 10).

Note

The measurements given for positioning the buttons indicate the center of each button.

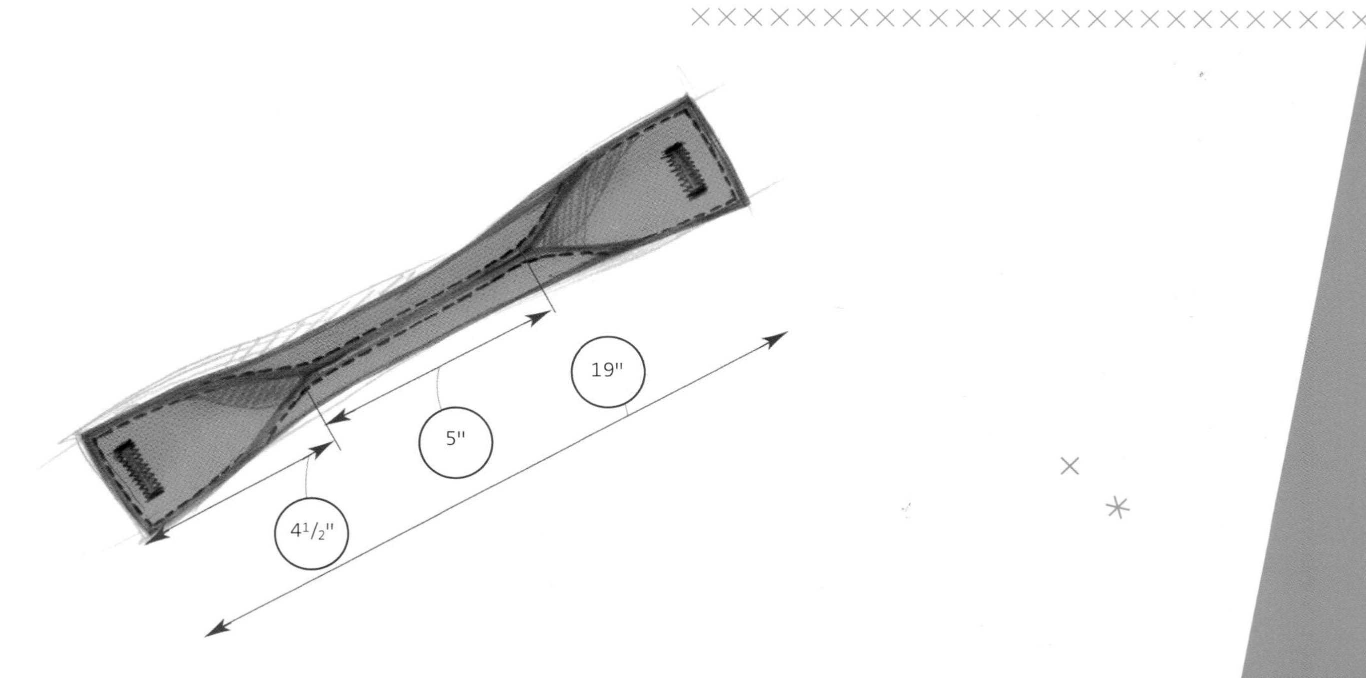

Prepare the pieces

Turn to page 143 to see how to position the pieces on the fabric.

Fake fur - Mark and then cut 1 piece to the size indicated in the materials list.

Striped silk - Mark and then cut:
1 piece 11¾" x 32" (29.5 cm x 80.5 cm);
1 strap 1¾" x 41" (4.5 cm x 104 cm).
Serge or zigzag the edges of the fake fur and silk pieces.

Gimp braid - Cut:
2 strap pieces 41" (104 cm) long;
1 cloverleaf closure piece 17" (43 cm) long;
1 button piece 7" (18 cm) long.

Interfacing - Mark and then cut 1 piece to the size indicated in the materials list.

1 On one short edge of the fake fur, fold 1¼" (3 cm) to the wrong side; pin and then sew ¼" (5 mm) from the serged edge. On the opposite edge, fold ¾" (1.5 cm) to the wrong side; pin and sew ¼" (5 mm) from the serged edge. To form the pouch section, fold this same end 10" (26 cm) to the right side. Pin together the serged edges on each side of the pouch; baste and then sew, using ½" (1 cm) seam allowance. At the end of each seam next to the fold, trim the seam allowance at an angle. Fold the serged edges of the flap ½" (1 cm) to the wrong side, folding them over the hem at the end. Pin and then slipstitch the edges to the flap (see fig. 16, page 16). Turn the bag right side out.

Tsarina bag

Dimensions: 11" (28 cm) wide x 10" (26 cm) high (excluding the strap)

Tools

Sewing essentials (see page 7),
Felt-tip marker with nonpermanent ink,
Ballpoint pen,
Household scissors,
Cutting mat,
Ruler,
Rotary cutter,
Craft glue.

Materials

- Charcoal brown fake fur (faux mink): 12" x 33" (30 cm x 83 cm)
- Yellow/antique-gold striped silk (for the lining; stripes parallel the longer edge): 13½" x 41" (34 cm x 104 cm)
- Antique-gold gimp braid, ½" (1.25 cm) wide: 3 yards (269 cm)
- Flexible interfacing (such as thin rubber sole from a shoe repair shop): 11" x 10" (28 cm x 25 cm)
- Thread: charcoal brown, antique-gold

2 To make the lining, repeat step 1 with the larger piece of striped silk; instead of hemming the edges, just fold and press the allowance to the wrong side; for the pouch, fold back 9¾" (25.5 cm) instead of 10" (26 cm).

3 On both long edges of the strap, fold and press ⅜" (1 cm) to the wrong side. Place the strap wrong side up, pin the two lengths of braid side-by-side on top of it, covering the folded margins. Baste; then sew the braid to the strap close to each outside edge. Slipstitch the adjacent edges of the braid together (see fig. 16, page 16).

4 Make sure the fake fur bag is right side out and the lining is wrong side out. Insert the lining in the fake fur bag, aligning the side seams. Slide the interfacing (all the way down) between the fabrics in the back of the pouch. Pin the folded edges of the lining over the hemmed edges of the fur. Slide the ends of the strap between the lining and fur, just above the pouch (the braid-trimmed side should face you); make sure the strap is not twisted. Slipstitch the lining to the fake fur. Secure the strap with small, inconspicous stitches that go through all the layers.

5 Before shaping the braid into the cloverleaf closure, seal the ends with glue so they do not fray; let the glue dry. Then follow the drawing below to shape the closure: Pin the layers of the braid one on top of the other in the sequence indicated, holding them in place with a few drops of glue as you work; then sew them by hand.

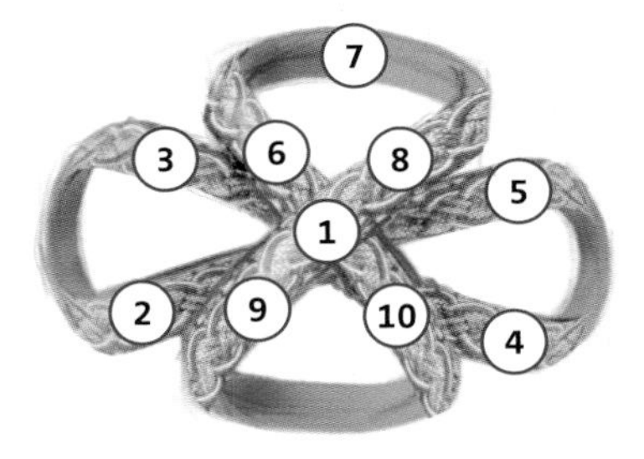

6 At each end of the braid for the button, fold ½" (1.5 cm) to the wrong side and secure with a drop of glue; let dry. Follow the drawing below to shape one end into a knotted button; secure the shape with invisible hand stitches.

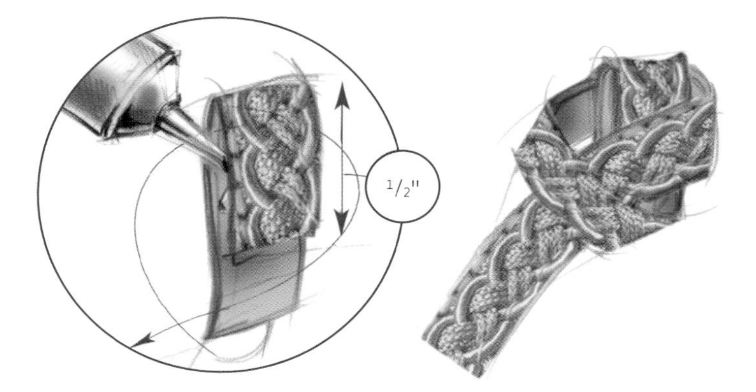

7 Center the cloverleaf closure on the fur side of the flap, with one loop extending over the edge; sew the closure to the fur by hand. Referring to the photos, position the button on the pouch; sew the edges of the braid to the fur.

Tools

Sewing essentials (see page 7),
Felt-tip marker with nonpermanent ink,
Grommet setting tool,
Gripper-snap setting tool.

Materials

- Floral-print heavy cotton: 22" x 40" (56 cm x 100 cm)
- Striped heavy cotton: 20" x 40" (51 cm x 100 cm), with the stripes parallel to the longer edge
- 8 gripper snaps, 1/2" (1.3 cm) in diameter
- 8 grommets, 1" (2.5 cm) in diameter
- 4 snap hooks
- Thread to match fabric

Picadilly Circus

Dimensions: 17 1/2" (45 cm) wide x 16 1/2" (42 cm) high (excluding the handles)

Prepare the pieces

Turn to page 143 to see how to arrange the pieces on your fabric.

Floral fabric - Mark and then cut:
2 main pieces 18 1/2" x 20" (47 cm x 50 cm);
2 handles 3 1/2" x 18 1/2" (9 cm x 47 cm).

Striped fabric - Mark and then cut:
2 main pieces 18 1/2" x 20" (47 cm x 50 cm);
4 handle links 1 1/2" x 7 1/2" (4 cm x 19 cm).

Serge or zigzag the edges of each piece.

1 Place the main pieces of floral fabric right sides together. Pin the layers together along the bottom (shorter) edge and both sides. Sew, using 1/2" (1 cm) seam allowance. Diagonally trim the seam allowance at the bottom corners. Press the seam allowances open. Turn the bag right side out.

2 Box one bottom corner of the bag by aligning the side seam on the bottom seam, forming a triangle. Centering it over the aligned seams, position the female half of a gripper snap about 1" (2 cm) from the point (make sure the decorative face is on the bottom of the bag), and affix it through all layers (see page 11); affix the male half about 5" (13 cm) farther along the side seam. Repeat the process on the other bottom corner. Then fold and press 1/2" (1 cm) to the wrong side along the top edge of the bag.

3 Repeat steps 1 and 2 with the striped fabric to make the reverse side of the bag.

4 Make sure the floral bag is right side out and the striped bag wrong side out. Insert the striped bag in the floral bag, aligning the side seams and top edges. Pin and then sew the top edges together, stitching close to the edge.

5 Mark the positions for the grommets 5" (12 cm) on each side of both side seams, marking one 1½" (4 cm) and another 5" (12 cm) below the top edge. Apply a grommet at each mark (see page 12); then fold down the top of the bag so that the pairs of grommets align.

6 On both long edges of each handle link strip, fold and press ⅜" (1 cm) to the wrong side. One at a time, thread each strip through a pair of grommets as shown in the drawing below; then, with the right sides together, align the ends and sew them together form a loop. Open the seam allowance and then fold the strip in half lengthwise with the right side out; pin, baste, and sew close to the long edges—you'll have to rotate the loop and push the bag away from the presser foot as you sew.

7 On all edges of each handle, fold and press ⅜" (1 cm) to the wrong side. Fold each handle in half lengthwise, right side out. Pin each handle closed along the open edges; then topstitch all around through all layers, stitching close to the edge.

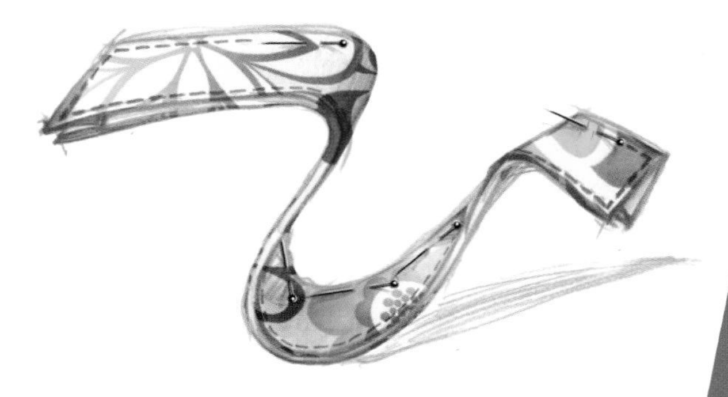

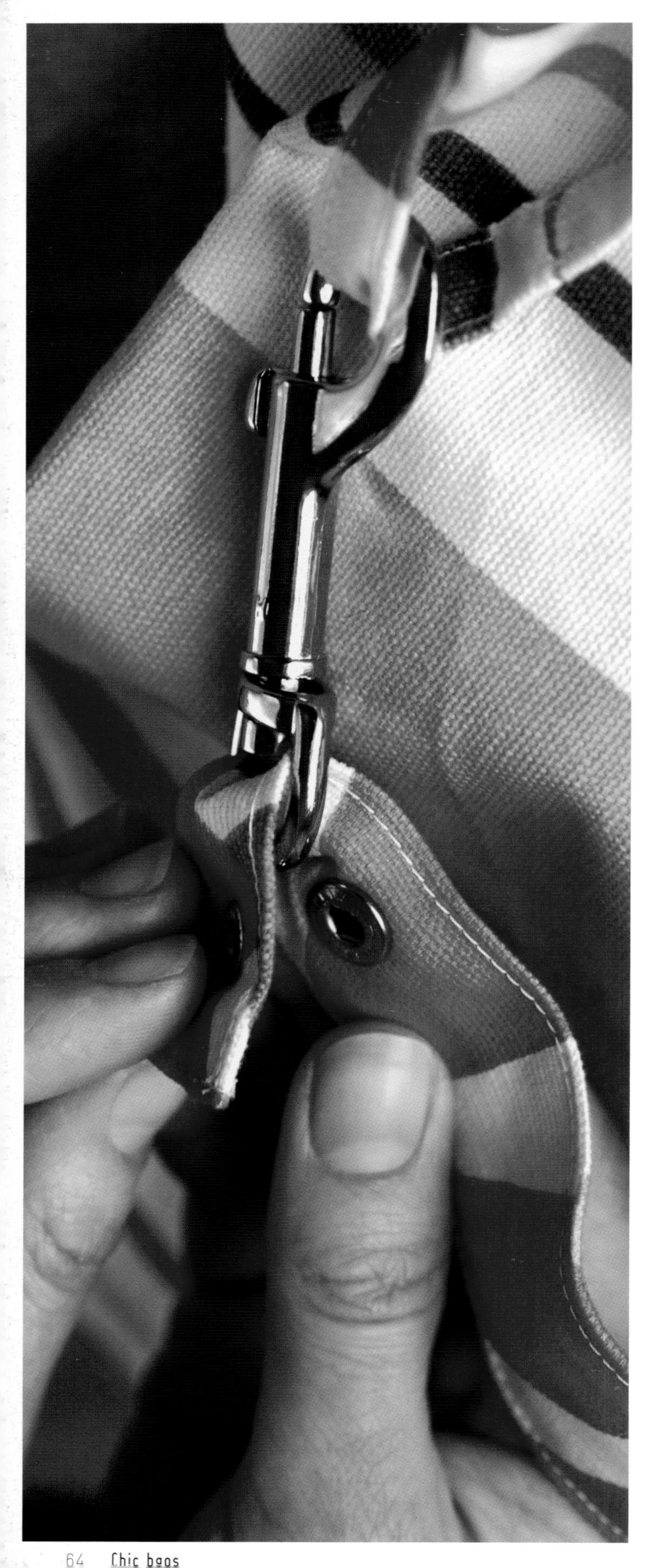

8 Insert one end of each handle through the ring end of a snap hook; using inconspicous hand stitches, securely sew the handle to itself, enclosing the metal bar.

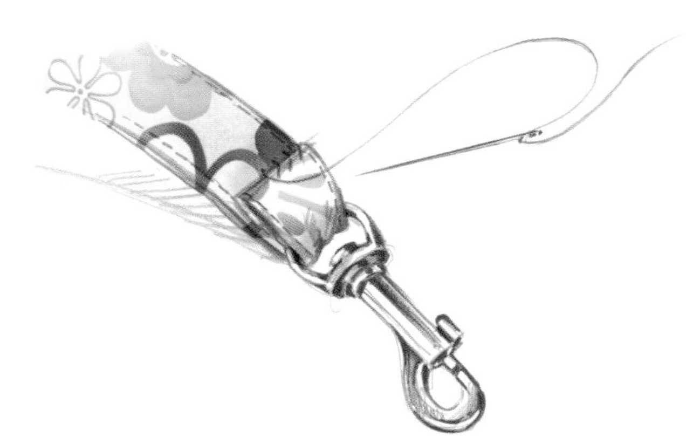

9 Turn each handle so the side with the folded-over allowance faces up. Referring to the drawing below, affix one male gripper snap half close to the loose end and two female snap halves at the intervals indicated. Insert the loose end of each strap through one of the remaining snap hooks; then snap it to the desired length. Clip the handles to the loops on the bag.

Tip

For sturdy results, use heavy-duty thread instead of regular sewing thread to assemble the bag–the seams will support more weight.

Note

The measurements given for positioning the snaps and grommets indicate the center of each snap or grommet.

Prepare the pieces

Copy the actual-size pattern for the main piece on page 144.

Turn to page 138 to see how to position the pieces on your fabric.

Printed cotton - Mark and then cut:
2 main pieces;
1 gusset 2" x 18" (5 cm x 49 cm);
4 handle links 1½" x 3¼" (4 cm x 8 cm);
1 button cover 2½" (6 cm) in diameter.

Striped cotton - Mark and then cut:
2 main pieces;
1 gusset 2" x 18" (5 cm x 49 cm).
Serge or zigzag the edges of each piece.

Interfacing - Trace and then cut 2 main pieces.

1 To assemble the exterior of the bag (geometric print), with the wrong sides together, pin one long edge of the gusset to each main piece, centering the gusset on the bottom (longer) edge of the main pieces and aligning the top corners. Sew together, using ¼" (5 mm) seam allowance. Diagonally trim the seam allowance at the lower corners. Along the top edge, press ¼" (5 mm) to the wrong side.

2 Repeat step 1 using the corresponding striped fabric pieces to make the lining.

Dots and feathers

Dimensions: 6½" (17 cm) wide at base x 1½" (4 cm) deep x 5½" (14 cm) high (excluding the handles)

Tools

Sewing essentials (see page 7)
Felt-tip marker with nonpermanent ink,
Ballpoint pen,
Compass,
Household scissors,
Cutting mat,
Ruler,
Rotary cutter,
Safety pins.

Materials

- Gray geometric print cotton: 10" x 18" (24 cm x 49 cm)
- Gray striped cotton (for the lining): 10" x 18" (24 cm x 49 cm)
- 1 pair transparent plastic hoop handles, no more than 4½" (13 cm) wide at base, with a ⅝" (1.5 cm) eye in each end
- White maribou boa: 16" (40 cm) length
- Button form to cover, 1½" (4 cm) in diameter
- Stiff interfacing (such as stencil Mylar): 20" x 10" (51 cm x 26 cm)
- Thread: gray, transparent nylon

Photocopier or tracing paper for copying the pattern.

3 On both long edges of each handle link strip, fold and press ¼" (1 cm) to the wrong side. Then fold each strip in half lengthwise with the right side out; pin, baste, and sew close to the long edges. Insert a strip through the eye at each end of each handle; fold so the ends of the strip align and baste them together, enclosing the plastic bar.

4 Turn the geometric print bag right side out. Place the interfacing inside, against the corresponding main pieces. Make sure the lining is wrong side out and insert it in the bag, aligning the seams and top edges. Center a handle above one side of the bag and insert the links between the lining and interfacing; pin the links in place; repeat with the other handle on the other side of the bag. Pin and then sew the top edges of the exterior and lining together, stitching close to the edge through all layers.

5 Cover the button form with the fabric cut for that purpose (see page 10). Sew the button to one side of the bag, centering it about 2" (4.5 cm) below the top edge.

6 Pin the maribou boa around the top edge of the bag (outside the handles). Sew it in place by hand using the transparent nylon thread.

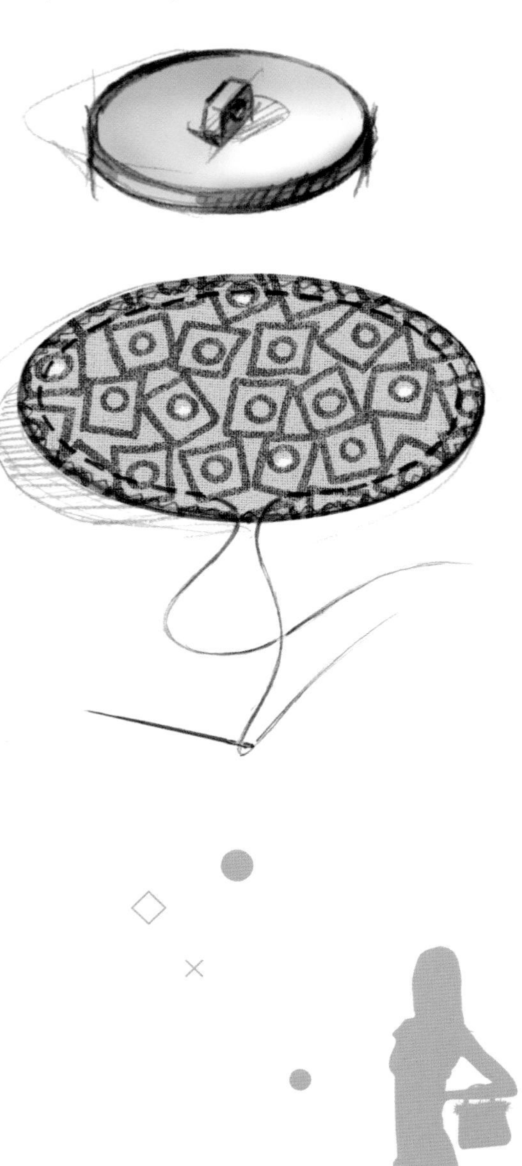

Tip

Wrap the cut ends of the maribou boa tightly with thread, or seal them with a drop of craft glue. When you put the boa on the bag, don't stretch it tightly, instead, let it fit naturally and slightly overlap the ends; use safety pins to secure the boa while you sew it on.

Tools

Sewing essentials (see page 7),
Felt-tip marker with nonpermanent ink,
Ballpoint pen,
Household scissors,
Cutting mat,
Ruler,
Rotary cutter.

Materials

- Blue denim: 33" x 36" (83 cm x 88 cm)
- Rabbit fur scarf, made with linked sections: approximately 32" (80 cm) long
- Cord for handles, 5/8" (1.5 cm) in diameter: 32" (80 cm)
- Thread: denim blue, transparent nylon
- Stiff interfacing (such as stencil Mylar): 23" x 14" (60 cm x 36 cm)

Be sure you have access to a photocopier for enlarging the pattern.

Denim with a fur collar

Dimensions: 10" (26 cm) wide x 4" (10 cm) deep x 10" (25 cm) high (excluding the handles)

Prepare the pieces

Photocopy the pattern on page 145, enlarging it to 135%.
Turn to page 145 to see how to position the pieces on your fabric.
Denim - Mark and then cut:
4 main pieces 15" x 11" (38 cm x 27 cm);
2 bottoms, adding 1/2" (1 cm) all around the pattern for seam allowance;
2 handles 3" x 18" (7 cm x 44 cm).
Serge or zigzag the edges of each piece.
Mark the center of each end on the wrong side of each bottom, as indicated by the black triangles on the pattern.
Interfacing - Mark and then cut:
1 bottom (do not add seam allowance),
2 main pieces 14" x 9 1/2" (36 cm x 25 cm).
Cord - Cut into two 16" (40 cm) lengths.

1 Place two of the denim main pieces right sides together. Pin and baste along the side (shorter) edges; then sew, using 1/2" (1 cm) seam allowance. Press the seam allowances open. Repeat to sew the two remaining denim main pieces together.

2 With the right sides together, pin one of the denim bottoms into one of the denim tubes made in step 1, aligning the marks on the bottom with the side seams. Sew, using 1/2" (1 cm) seam allowance. Notch the seam allowances along the curves, then press them open. Sew the remaining denim bottom and tube together and open the seams in the same way.

3 Fold and press 1/2" (1 cm) to the wrong side along the top of each bag.

4 Fold and press 1/2" (1 cm) to the wrong side on one long edge of each handle. Center a piece of cord lengthwise on the wrong side of each. Wrap the fabric over the cord, lapping the folded edge (B) over the cut edge (A) and pinning the layers snugly together. Slipstitch the layers together (see fig. 16, page 16).

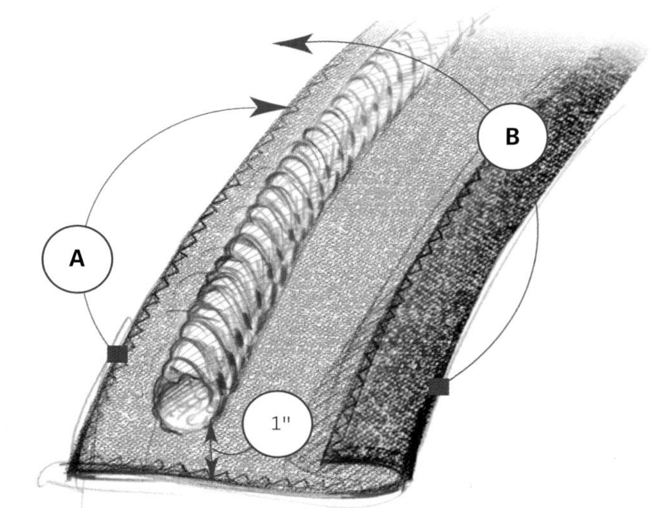

5 Turn one of the bags right side out. Place the interfacing bottom inside it. Make sure the other bag is wrong side out and insert it in the first, aligning the side seams and top edges. Slide the interfacing main pieces between the bags, aligning the edges with the seams and the turned-in top allowance. Pin the rabbit fur scarf temporarily around the top edge of the bag, centering its ends on one side. Curve one of the handles above one side of the bag and insert the ends between the denim layers, placing each end about 4 1/4" (11 cm) from a side seam and extending it 1" (2 cm) below the top; pin. Repeat with the other handle on the other side of the bag. Remove the scarf. Pin the top edges of the bags together, sew close the edge; hand-sew the edges to the handles securely, stitching all the way through each to trap the cord ends.

Tip

For sturdy results, use heavy-duty thread instead of regular sewing thread to assemble the bag–the seams will support more weight.

6 Reposition the fur scarf on the top edge of the bag, adjusting the links to drape softly. Pin it in place; then, using nylon thread, sew it loosely to the denim with inconspicuous stitches.

Carry-along shopping tote

Tote dimensions: 16" (40 cm) wide x 5" (12 cm) deep x 21" (55 cm) high (handles included)

Case dimensions: 4" (10 cm) wide x 6¾" (16 cm) high

Tools

Sewing essentials (see page 7),
Felt-tip marker with nonpermanent ink,
Household scissors,
Embroidery needle.

Materials

- Dark pink lightweight cotton: 30" x 42" (62 cm x 106 cm)
- Light pink lightweight cotton: 30" x 42" (62 cm x 106 cm)
- Dark pink button, ¾" (2 cm) in diameter
- Thread: dark pink, light pink
- Light pink pearl cotton, size 5

Be sure you have access to a photocopier for enlarging the pattern.

Prepare the pieces

Photocopy the half-pattern on page 146, enlarging it to 229%. Make a second copy of the upper portion only for the facing.

Turn to page 146 to see how to position the pieces on your fabric. Be sure to fold the fabric as shown for cutting the main piece and facing (see fig. 8, page 14).

From both fabrics, mark and then cut:

1 main piece, adding ½" (1 cm) on all edges except the fold;

1 facing, adding ½" (1 cm) on all edges except the fold;

1 gusset 3½" x 42" (8 cm x 106 cm);

1 carrying case 5" x 8" (12 cm x 19 cm).

Mark the bottom center (the fold) on the wrong side of each main piece; mark the midpoint of the long edges on the wrong side of the gusset.

Tote bag

1 On each main piece and facing, pin the ends of the handles right sides together as shown in the drawing below. Sew, using ½" (1 cm) seam allowance. Press the seam allowances open.

To keep the seams flat, topstitch through all layers on both sides of each seam, stitching close to the seam.

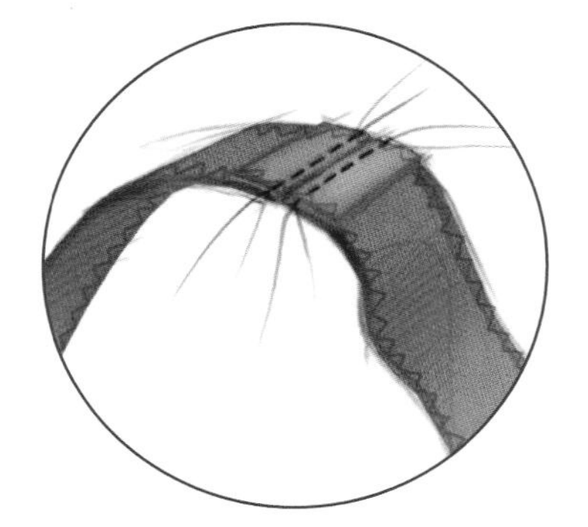

2 With the right sides together and corresponding edges aligned, place the light pink facing on the dark pink main piece. Pin together around the inside of the handle; sew, using 1/2" (1 cm) seam allowance. Clip the seam allowance along the curves. Turn the piece right side out; press the seamed edge. Topstitch close to the seam through all layers. Repeat to assemble the dark pink facing and the light pink main piece.

3 At one end of one of the pieces just sewn, turn the layers to be right sides together. Pin along the top edge (toward the handle) for a short way, then using 1/2" (1 cm) allowance, sew where pinned for 2" (5 cm). Repeat at the other end of this piece and both ends of the other piece.

4 Place the two gussets right sides together. Pin and then, with light pink thread, sew together along one of the long edges, using 1/2" (1 cm) seam allowance. Press the allowances open; then press them together onto the darker piece, folding under 1/4" (5 mm) along the edge as you go. Baste through all layers; then, using dark pink thread, topstitch close to the fold.

5 With the right sides together and beginning by matching the center marks, pin the dark pink half of the gusset to the light pink main piece: Pin from the center out; when you reach the facing, lift it away from the main piece (fold the seam allowance toward the facing) and pin the gusset to it. Baste and then sew, using 1/2" (1 cm) seam allowance. Pin and then sew the light pink half of the gusset to the dark pink main piece in the same way.

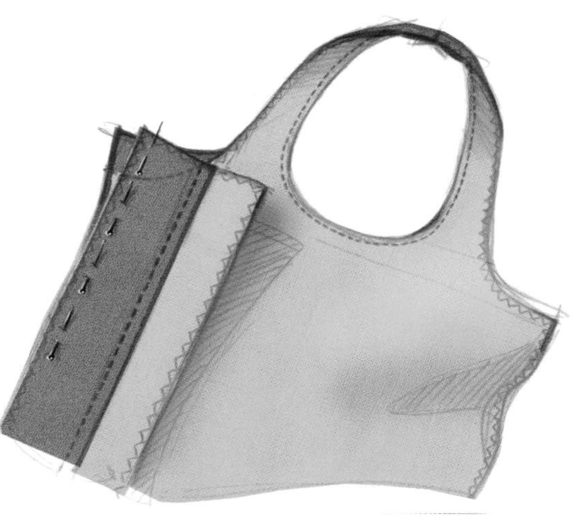

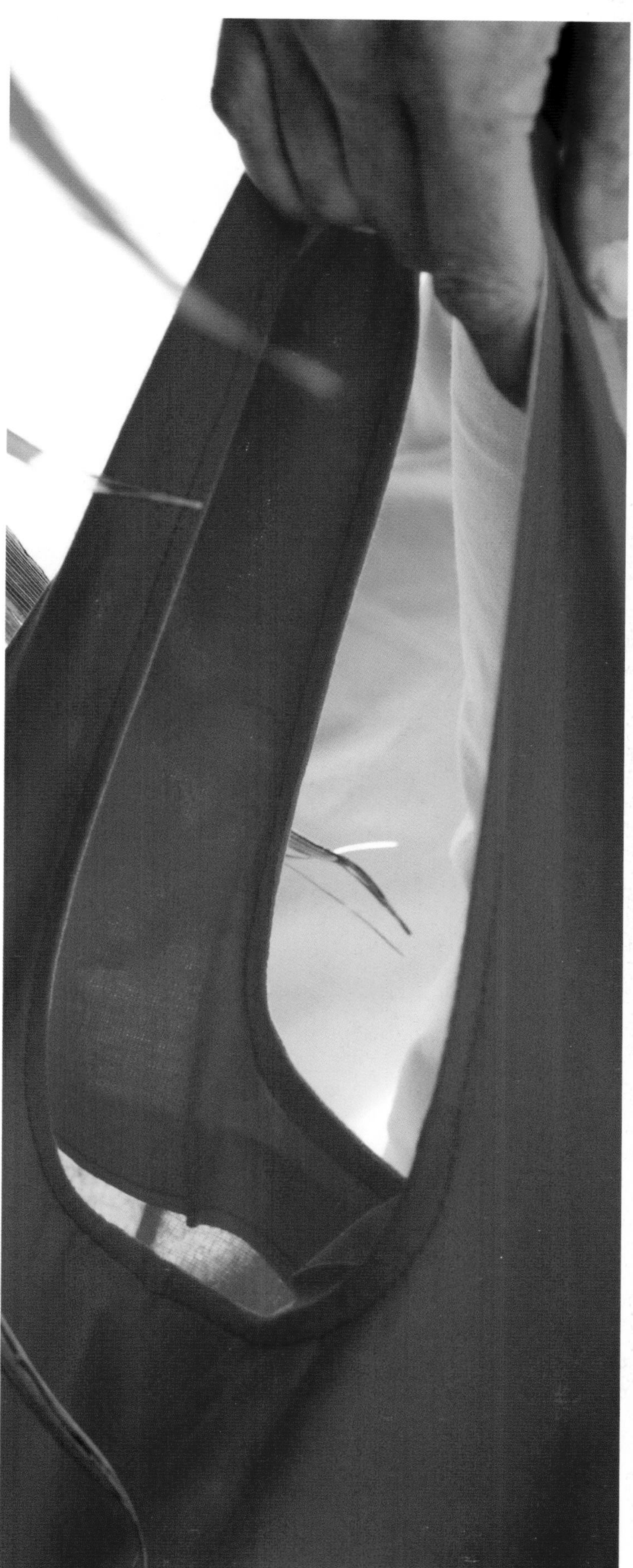

6 Fold the facing to the inside again, folding the top of each gusset to the inside between the seams made in step 3; press. To complete the rest of the top edge, fold 1/2" (1 cm) to the wrong side on each layer, pressing as you go; pin and baste the layers together (the seam allowance should be between the facing and main pieces). Topstitch close to the edge all around the top (including the handles), using thread to match each section.

7 Lift the facing and press 1/2" (1 cm) to the wrong side all along the lower edge, including across the gusset ends. Stitch close to the edge (keep the facing free; don't stitch it to the bag). If you like, tack the facing edge to the side seams.

Carrying case

1 Place the case pieces right sides together. Pin the layers together along the bottom (narrower) edge and both sides. Sew, using 1/2" (1 cm) seam allowance. Diagonally trim the seam allowance at the bottom corners.

2 Fold and press 5/8" (1.5 cm) to the wrong side along the top edge; repeat. Pin and then sew through all layers 3/8" (1 cm) from the top edge, using thread to match each section.

3 Referring to the photo at right and using the pearl cotton, make a thread link button loop at the top center of the dark pink side; make it about 5/8" (1.5 cm) wide and 1 1/2" (4 cm) long (see fig. 19 and 20, page 16). Using the pearl cotton, sew the button to the light pink side, centering it 1" (2.5 cm) below the top edge.

Because this bag is unlined, it's essential to finish the edges of the fabric with a serger or zigzag stitch.

For professional results, change thread as needed to match each piece you are sewing–use a bobbin thread that matches the fabric against the feeddogs and a top thread that matches the fabric against the presser foot.

Tools

Sewing essentials (see page 7),

Felt-tip pen with nonpermanent ink,
Pencil,
Cutting mat,
Rotary cutter,
Ruler,
Zipper foot for your sewing machine.

Materials

- Striped heavyweight cotton: 18" x 40" (46 cm x 98 cm)
- Red heavyweight cotton (for the lining): 18" x 23" (46 cm x 58 cm)
- 1 pair brown leather handles, fitted at each end with a metal ring 1¼" (3 cm) in diameter
- Medium-weight cardboard (for stiffener): 22" x 14" (55 cm x 36 cm)
- Turquoise ribbon, ½" (1 cm) wide: 11" (26 cm)
- Turquoise ribbon, 1" (2 cm) wide: 8" (16 cm)
- Metal ring, 1" (2 cm) in diameter
- Snap hook
- Sew-on magnetic snap closure (or large conventional snap)
- Thread: to match striped fabric, red

Summer stripe

Tote dimensions: 14″ (36 cm) wide x 2″ (6 cm) deep x 11″ (25 cm) high (excluding the handles)
Detachable pocket dimensions: 7″ (18 cm) wide x 4″ (11.5 cm) high

Prepare the pieces

Turn to page 147 to see how to position the pieces on your fabric.

Striped cotton - Mark and then cut:
1 main piece 15" x 23" (38 cm x 58 cm);
2 gussets 3" x 11" (8 cm x 27 cm);
1 detachable pocket 8" x 17" (20 cm x 40 cm).

Red cotton - Mark and then cut:
1 main piece 15" x 23" (38 cm x 58 cm);
2 gussets 3" x 11" (8 cm x 27 cm).

Serge or zigzag the edges of each piece.
On the wrong side of the fabric, mark the midpoint of both long edges of each main piece and the midpoint of one end of each gusset.

Narrower ribbon - Cut one 8" (20 cm) and one 3" (6 cm) length.

Wider ribbon - Cut four 2" (4 cm) lengths.

Cardboard - Mark and then cut:
1 bottom 2" x 14" (6 cm x 36 cm);
2 sides 14" x 10½" (36 cm x 24.5 cm).

c'est une

une

Tote

1 Referring to the drawing below, place the striped fabric pieces right sides together, matching the mark on the end of each gusset to a mark on the edge of the main piece; then, working out from the midpoint toward the top on both edges, pin each gusset to the edge of the main piece. Sew, using $^1/_2$" (1 cm) seam allowance.

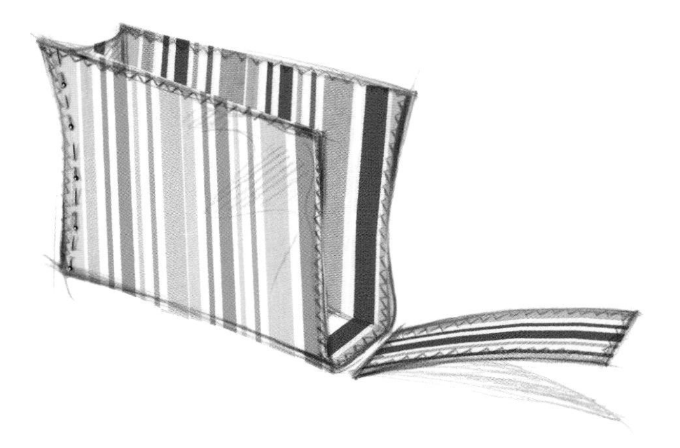

Diagonally trim the seam allowance at the bottom corners. Fold and press $^1/_2$" (1 cm) to the wrong side on the top edge of the bag.

2 Pin together the lining pieces as explained in step 1. Before you sew, pass the longest piece of ribbon through the ring of the snap hook; bring the ends of the ribbon together and sew the long edges closed. Put the ribbon into the inside-out lining bag and slide the ends into one of the pinned seams about $2^1/_2$" (6 cm) below the top.

Sew the lining as pinned, using $^1/_2$" (1 cm) seam allowance. Fold and press $^1/_2$" (1 cm) to the wrong side along the top edge of the bag.

3 Turn the striped bag right side out. Insert the cardboard bottom. Make sure the lining is wrong side out and insert it in the bag, aligning the seams and top edges. Slide a cardboard piece between the lining and outside on each broad side of the bag; make sure the top of the cardboard sits below the turned down top allowance.

4 Referring to the drawing below, pass the wider ribbons through the rings at the handle ends; fold each ribbon in half to enclose its ring. Curve the handles above the sides of the bag and insert the ribbon ends between the fabric layers, placing each about 3" (8 cm) from a gusset seam; pin. Pin and then baste the top edges of the bags together. Using the zipper foot, sew along the top edge of each broad side of the bag. Sew the top edge of each gusset closed by hand.

Zire

Detachable pocket

1 On one end (shorter edge), fold and press 1/4" (1 cm) and then 1" (3 cm) to the wrong side. Sew through all layers close to the first fold. On the opposite end, fold and press 1/4" (1 cm) to the wrong side; turn the piece over and fold the same end 2" (6 cm) to the right side; press. On each long edge of the piece, sew the layers of this folded section together using 1/2" (1 cm) seam allowance. Trim the seam allowance at the corners. Turn the faced end just made right side out.

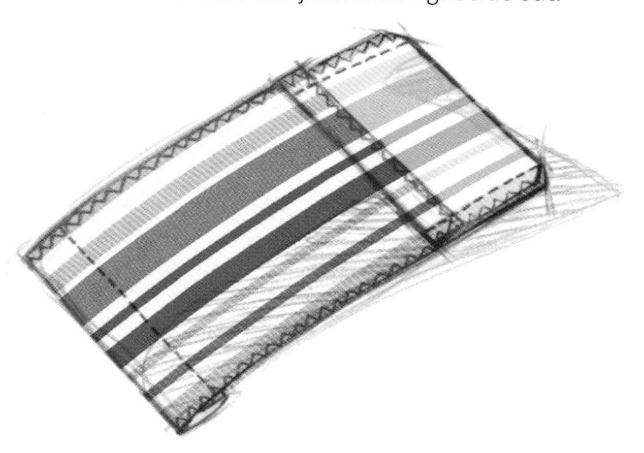

2 Press the faced end; also fold and press the seam allowances along the remaining edges to the wrong side. Topstitch the facing close to the loose edge through all layers. Make a pocket at the other end by folding the fabric wrong sides together, leaving a small space between the end and the facing. Fold the remaining piece of ribbon through the ring, bring the ends together and insert them between the layers on one side

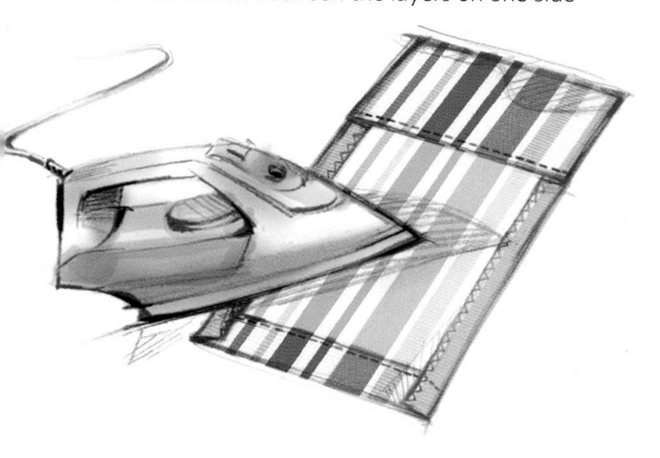

of the pocket so the ring extends. Pin the sides of the pocket closed; then sew close to each edge through all layers, reinforcing the top corners with a small triangle (see fig. 23, page 17).

3 Fold the faced end over the pocket. Decide the best place for the snap; mark on each section. Sew one half of the snap to each section (sew through only one layer of each so the pocket stays open and no stitches show on the flap).

Tip

To sew the top of the bag, use bobbin thread that matches the outside of the bag and thread that matches the lining in the needle; sew with the outside of the bag against the feed dogs.

Prepare the pieces

Photocopy the pattern on page 148, enlarging it to 118%. *Turn to page 148 to see how to position the pieces on your fabric.*

Damask - Mark and then cut:
2 main pieces 14½" x 10" (36 cm x 25 cm);
1 bottom, adding ½" (1 cm) all around;
2 handles 2" x 18" (5 cm x 44 cm).

Velveteen - Mark and then cut:
2 main pieces 14½" x 10" (36 cm x 25 cm);
1 bottom, adding ½" (1 cm) all around.

Serge or zigzag the edges of each piece. On the wrong side of both bottom pieces, mark the midpoint of both longer edges as indicated by the black triangles on the pattern (first decide which side of the damask you wish to use as the right side of the bottom).

Interfacing - Mark and cut 1 bottom; don't add seam allowance.

PVC tube - Cut into two 16" (40 cm) lengths.

1 Place the damask main pieces one on top of the other with their opposite sides together (so that each half of the bag will be a different tone). Pin the layers together along the shorter edges; then sew, using ½" (1 cm) seam allowance. Press the seam allowances open. Topstitch through both layers on each side of each seam, stitching close to the seam.

Theater or opera?

Dimensions: 11" (27 cm) wide x 5" (12 cm) deep x 9" (23 cm) high (excluding the handles)

Tools

Sewing essentials (see page 7),
Felt-tip pen with nonpermanent ink,
Ballpoint pen,
Household scissors,
Cutting mat,
Ruler,
Rotary cutter.

Materials

- Ecru floral damask (reversible): 35" x 14" (86 cm x 35 cm)
- Red velveteen: 35" x 12" (86 cm x 29 cm)
- Crisp interfacing (such as stencil Mylar): 11" x 5" (27 cm x 12 cm)
- PVC tube, ⅜" (1 cm) in diameter (for the handles, from a hardware or aquarium supply store): 32" (80 cm)
- Red twisted decorative cord, ⅜" (5 mm) in diameter: 12" (30 cm)
- Thread: ecru, red

Be sure you have access to a photocopier for enlarging the pattern.

2 With the right sides together, pin the bottom into the tube made in step 1, aligning the marks on the bottom with the seams of the tube. Sew, using ½" (1 cm) seam allowance. Notch the allowance on the curves.

3 With the right sides together in all cases, repeat steps 1 and 2 to assemble the velveteen lining (to keep it from crushing, press the velveteen with the right side against a towel). Along the top edge of both bags, fold and press ½" (1 cm) to the wrong side.

4 Fold and press ½" (1 cm) to the wrong side on one long edge of each handle. Center a tube lengthwise on the wrong side of each. Wrap the fabric over the tube, lapping the folded edge over the cut edge and pinning the layers snugly together. Slipstitch the layers together (see fig. 16, page 16).

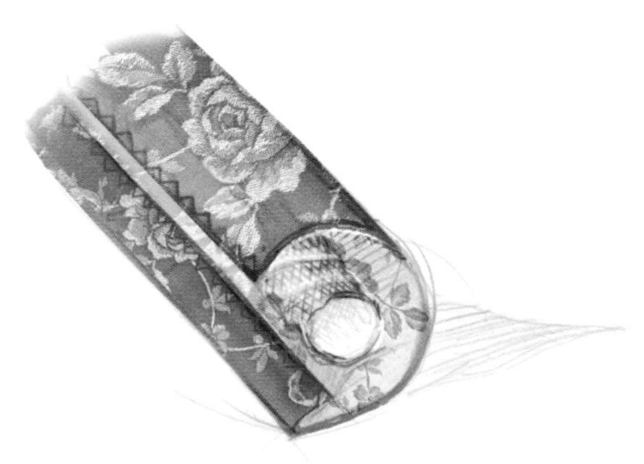

5 Tie a double knot about 1½" (3 cm) from each end of the decorative cord. Unravel each end to make a tassel; trim to even the ends.

6 Turn the damask bag right side out. Place the interfacing bottom inside it. Make sure the lining is wrong side out and insert it, aligning the seams and top edges. Curve a handle above each side, placing the handle ends about 3" (7.5 cm) from the seam and extending them 1" (2 cm) below the top; pin. Fold the decorative cord in half and insert the folded end between the layers next to one of the handles. Pin the top edges of the bags together. Slipstitch them closed; sew the edges to the handles securely, stitching all the way through each to trap the cord ends above the edge of the bag.

Tip

To give this bag a pretty roundness, interline it with lightweight batting. You can affix the batting to the wrong side of the lining with spray fabric glue.

7 To shape the top edge of the bag, gather it by hand with long, straight stitches (see fig. 13, page 16): Use doubled red thread, knot it, and then sew through all layers from handle to handle around each end of the bag, about 1" (2.5 cm) below the edge. Pull the thread to gather the fabric; then secure the thread with small stitches.

Tools

Sewing essentials (see page 7),

Felt-tip marker with nonpermanent ink,

Ballpoint pen,

Household scissors,

Zipper foot for your sewing machine.

Materials

- Coral fleece: 30" x 40" (76 cm x 100 cm)
- Dark brown leather: 3/4" x 4" (2 cm x 10 cm)
- Brown leather handle, fitted at each end with a metal ring 1 1/4" (3 cm) in diameter
- Coral zipper, 10" (25 cm) long
- Metal ring, 3/4" (2 cm) in diameter
- Lobster key fob (optional)
- Coral thread
- Contact cement or strong glue

All-terrain hobo

Dimensions: 13" (34 cm) wide x 15" (38 cm) high (excluding the handle)

Prepare the pieces

Photocopy the half-pattern on page 149, enlarging it to 166%.

Turn to page 149 to see how to arrange the pieces on your fabric. Be sure to fold the fabric as shown for cutting (see fig. 8, page 14).

Fleece - Mark and then cut:

4 main pieces;

2 handle links 3 1/2" x 3" (9 cm x 8 cm);

1 interior pocket 9" x 7" (21 cm x 16 cm).

Serge or zigzag the edges of each piece. On the wrong side of each main piece, mark the position of the zipper as indicated by the black triangles on the pattern.

Leather - Mark and then cut 2 pieces 3/8" x 4" (1 cm x 10 cm).

1 Place two of the main pieces right sides together. Pin and sew along the larger curved edge using 3/8" (1 cm) seam allowance; leave the top (smaller curve) open.

2 With the right sides together, pin the zipper to the top seam allowances of the bag assembled in step 1 (see fig. 6, page 12); the zipper should be open so you can turn the bag right side out later. Baste the zipper to the allowances, then sew it on using the zipper foot and stitching close to the edge.

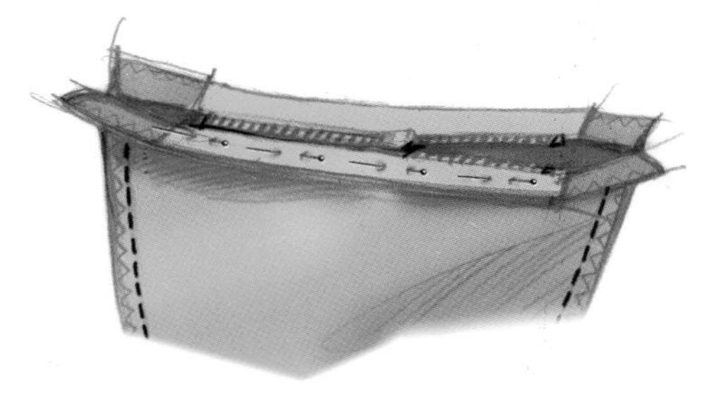

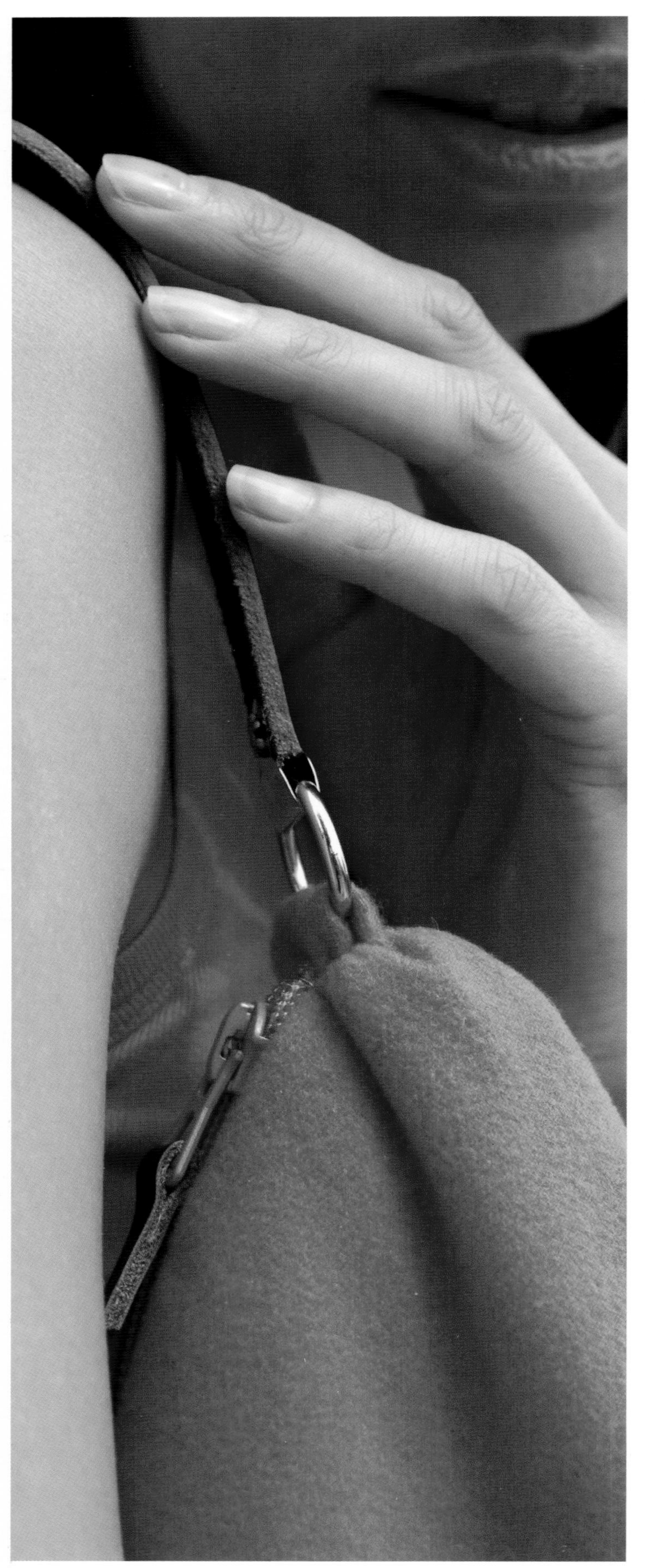

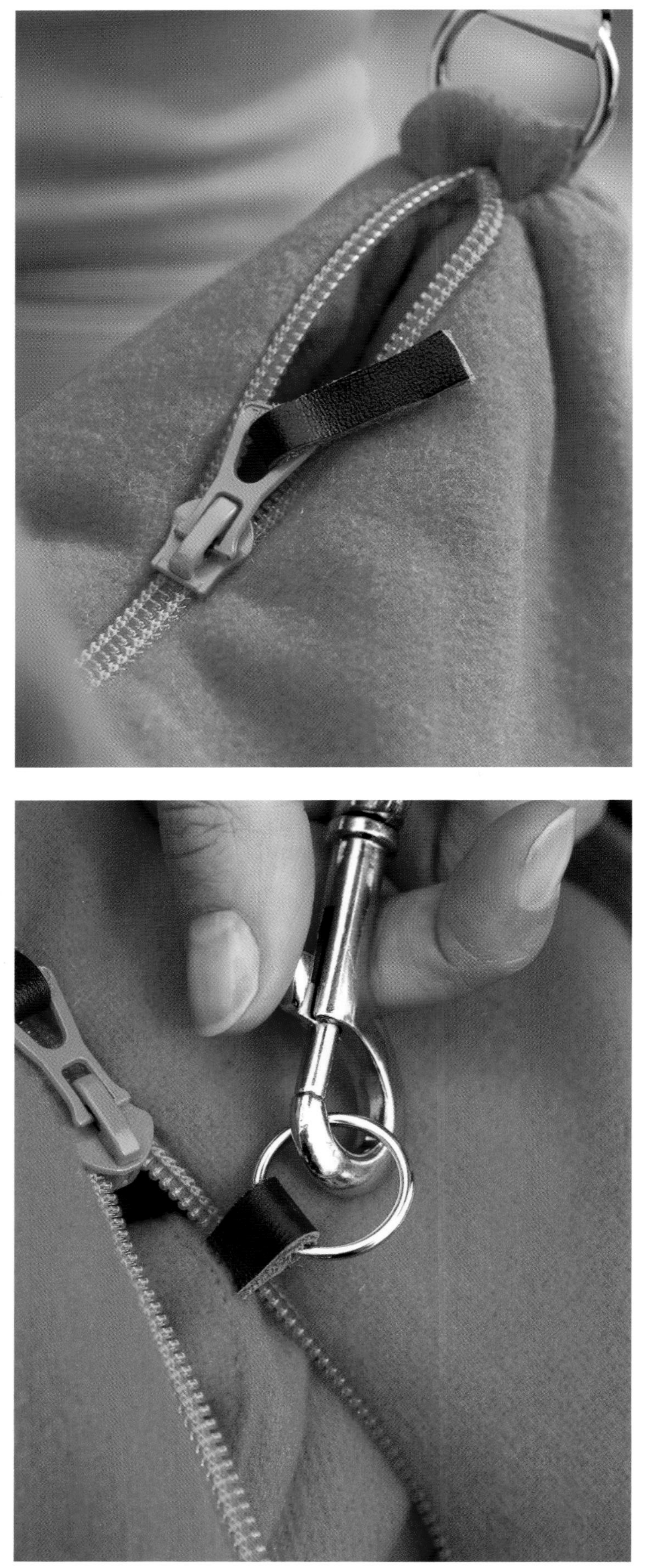

3 With the wrong side out, fold each handle link strip in half crosswise, bringing the shorter edges together. Pin and then sew, using 3/8" (1 cm) seam allowance, forming each into a tube. Press the seam allowances open. Referring to the drawing below, turn each tube right side out, centering the seam on the opposite face instead of on the edge; press lightly.

4 With the seam toward the metal bar, insert each strip through a ring at the end of the handle; fold so the ends of the strip align and pin them together, enclosing the metal bar. Sew a short distance from the edge.

5 Turn the bag with the zipper right side out, folding the top seam allowance to the inside. Curve the handle above the zipper, and insert the loop at each end into the bag, centering the loop on the side seam as shown in the drawing below. Baste the loop to the turned-in allowance.

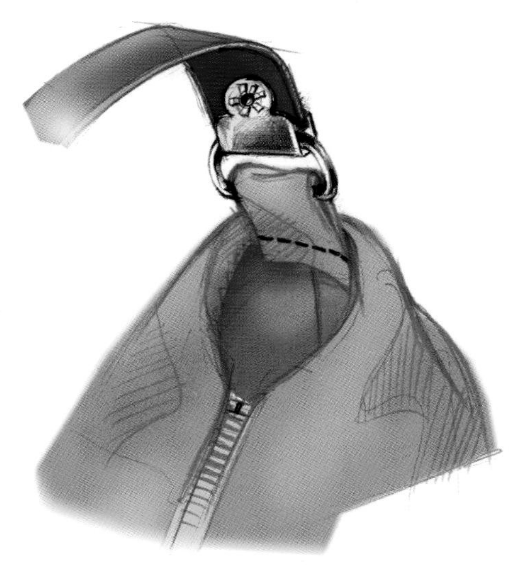

Then, referring to the photos and using doubled thread and long straight stitches, gather the open top edge at each end of the zipper by hand (see fig. 13, page 16); pull the thread to tighten the fabric around the handle link and secure it with a few small stitches; then slipstitch the fabric to each handle link (see fig. 16, page 16).

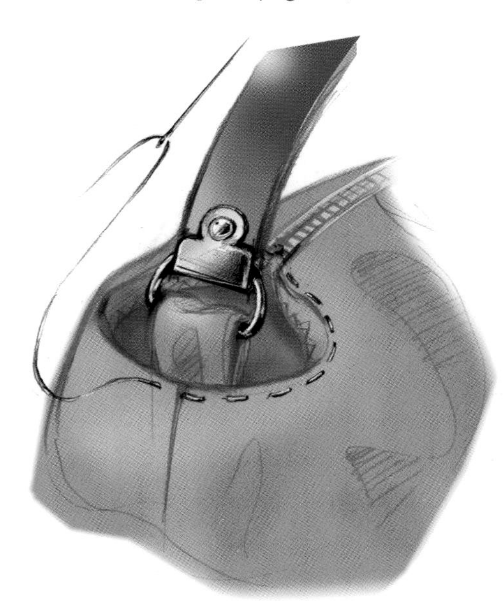

6 On the interior pocket, fold and press ½" (1 cm) to the wrong side along all edges. Topstitch one of the longer edges ¼" (1 cm) from the fold; this is the top of the pocket. Pin the pocket, right side up, to the right side of one of the remaining main pieces, centering it about 4½" (12 cm) above the bottom curve. Insert one of the small leather strips through the metal ring, fold it so the ends of the strip align, and then insert the ends under one edge of the pocket, about 2" (5 cm) from the top, with the ring extending as shown in the drawing at right. Topstitch the pocket in place, making two parallel rows of stitching along the side and bottom edges.

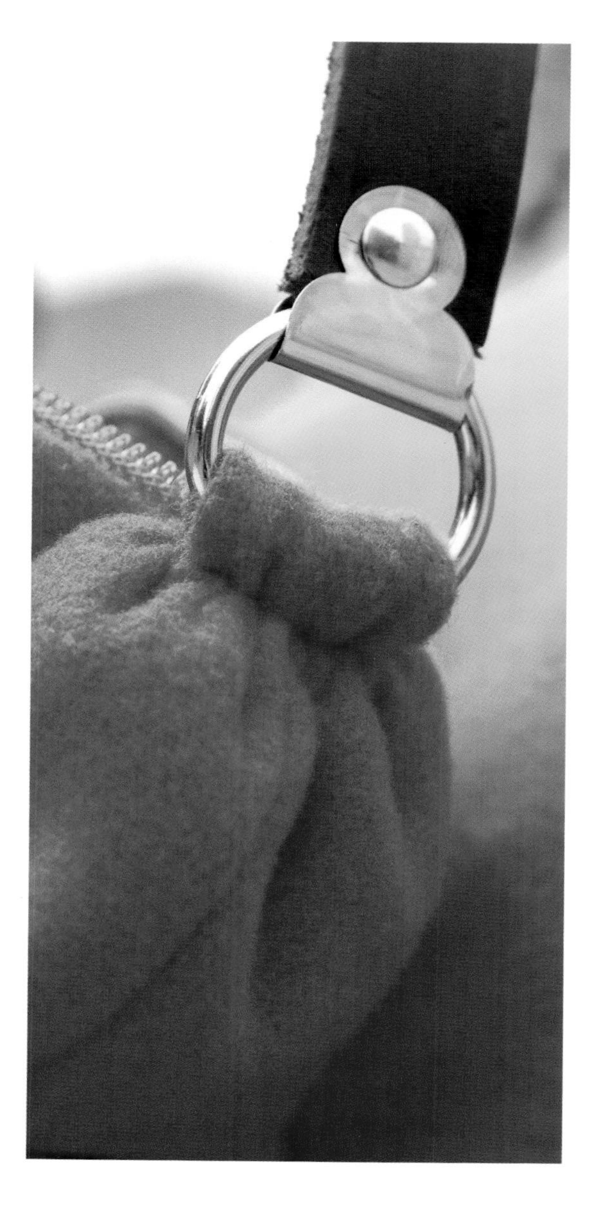

7 To make the lining, repeat step 1 to sew the remaining main piece to the piece with the pocket. Press the seam allowances open.

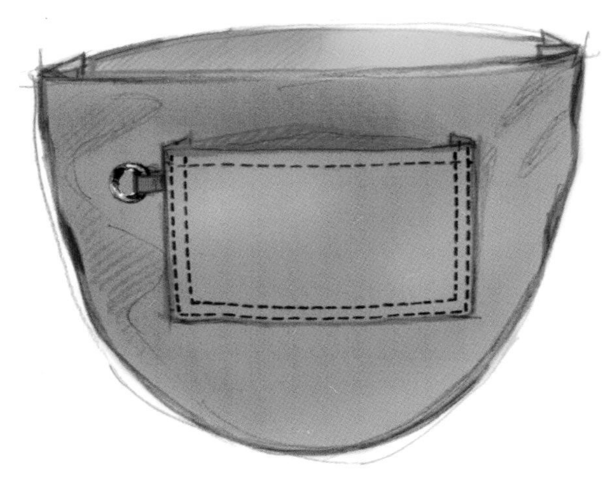

8 Fold and press ½" (1 cm) to the wrong side along the top of the lining. Turn the lining right side out. Turn the bag with the zipper wrong side out (through the open zipper) and insert it into the lining, aligning the seams. Pin the top edge of the lining to the zipper tape, being sure to leave room for the zipper slide to move easily. Slipstitch the lining to the zipper tape. Gather and secure the edges at each end of the zipper as you did in step 5. Turn the bag right side out.

9 Insert the remaining strip of leather through the zipper pull. Apply glue to the wrong side of the strip ends; let dry for 20 minutes. Then press the strip ends together, enclosing the bar of the pull. Clip the key fob onto the ring on the inside pocket if you wish.

Clever bucket bag

Bag dimensions: 10" (25.5 cm) in diameter x 20 1/2" (52 cm) high
Detachable pocket dimensions: 17" (18 cm) wide x 5" (13 cm) high

Tools

Sewing essentials (see page 7), Felt-tip marker with nonpermanent ink, Compass, Household scissors, Cutting mat, Ruler Rotary cutter, Leather needle, Thimble, Gripper-snap setting tool.

Materials

- Light gray industrial felt, 1/4" (5 mm) thick: 33" x 24" (80 cm x 58 cm)
- Pink cotton broadcloth: 34" x 18" (82 cm x 42 cm)
- Pink cotton cord or pink rattail, 1/8" (3 mm) in diameter: 1 yd (90 cm)
- 2 gripper snaps with silver-color caps, 1/2" (1.3 cm) in diameter
- Snap hook
- Pink thread
- Pink pearl cotton, size 3
- Contact cement or strong glue

Be sure you have access to a photocopier for enlarging the patterns.

Prepare the pieces

Photocopy the patterns on pages 150 and 151, enlarging the one for the main piece to 228% and the one for the bottom to 200%. *Turn to page 150 to see how to arrange the pieces on your fabric; to complete the half-pattern for the main piece, reverse it as shown.*

Felt - Mark and then cut:
1 main piece; 1 bottom; 4 hearts.

Cotton - Mark and then cut:
1 drawstring insert 34" x 8" (82 cm x 18 cm);
1 detachable pocket 8" x 19" (20 cm x 45 cm);
1 snap hook strap 2" x 16" (4 cm x 40 cm).
Serge or zigzag the edges of each piece of cotton.

Cord - Cut one 33" (82 cm) length for the bag and one 3" (8 cm) length for the pocket.

Detachable pocket

1 On one short edge of the pocket, fold and press 1/2" (1 cm) twice to the wrong side. On the opposite edge, fold and press 1/2" (5 mm) and then 1 1/2" (3 cm) to the wrong side; pin and then sew through all layers close to the first fold. Turn the piece over and fold the stitched end 5" (13 cm) to the right side; pin.

Fold the shorter piece of cord in half; slide it, folded end in, between the layers on one edge of the doubled end just formed; align the cord ends with the edge of the fabric. Fold up the opposite end of the fabric, overlapping it slightly on the stitched hem as shown below. Sew each open edge through all layers using 1/2" (1 cm) seam allowance. Trim the allowance at each corner.

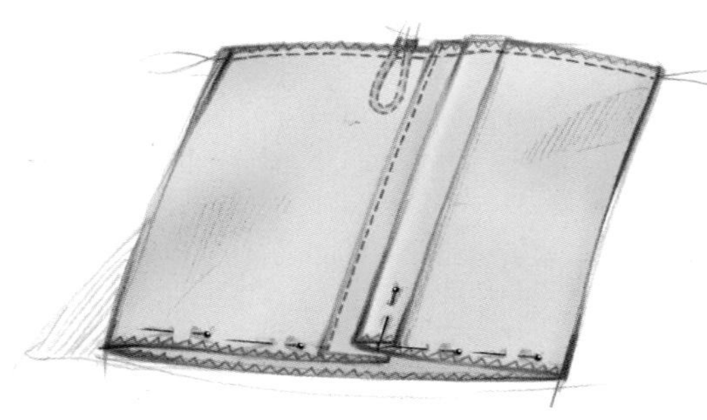

2 Turn the pocket right side out. Topstitch the flap (shallower end) close to the edges and across the inside hem. Affix the gripper snaps, placing a female portion on the flap 1/2" (3 cm) from each side and 3/8" (2 cm) from the end, as shown below, and a male portion opposite each on the inside of the pocket (see page 11).

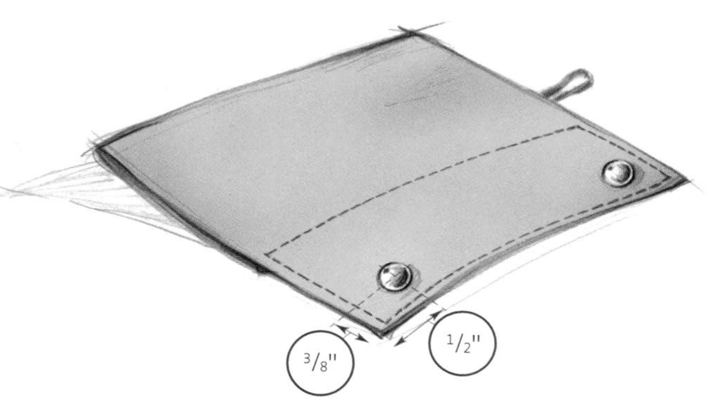

Note

The measurements given for positioning the gripper snaps indicate the center of each snap.

Bag

1 On the main piece, butt the ends of the handle; secure with safety pins. Hand-sew together, using pearl cotton and a large cross-stitch (see fig. 17, page 16); make each stitch all

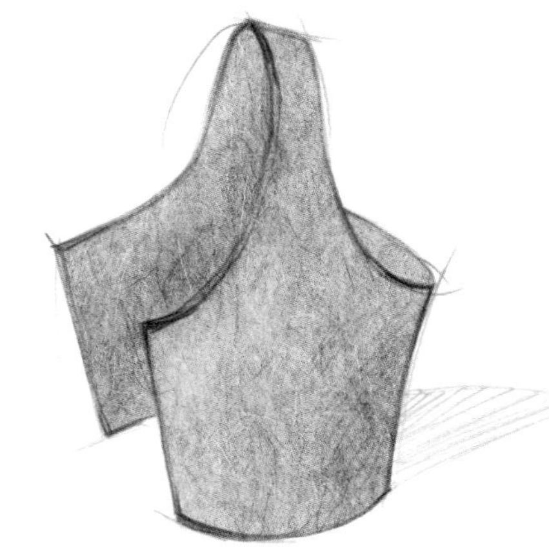

the way through the felt. Butt the side edges and sew together in the same way. With peal cotton, sew straight stitches all around the top opening/ handle, close to the edge (see fig. 13, page 16).

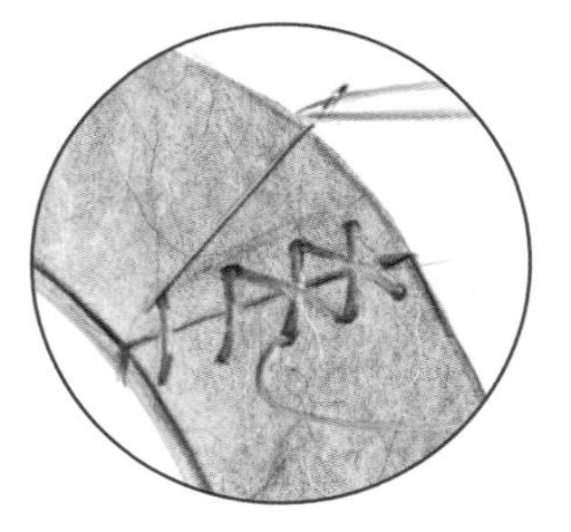

2 With the wrong sides together, pin the main piece to the bottom. Using pearl cotton and straight stitches, sew them together by hand.

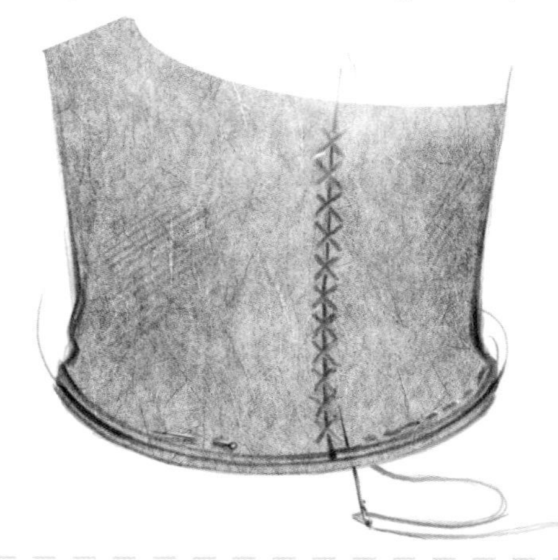

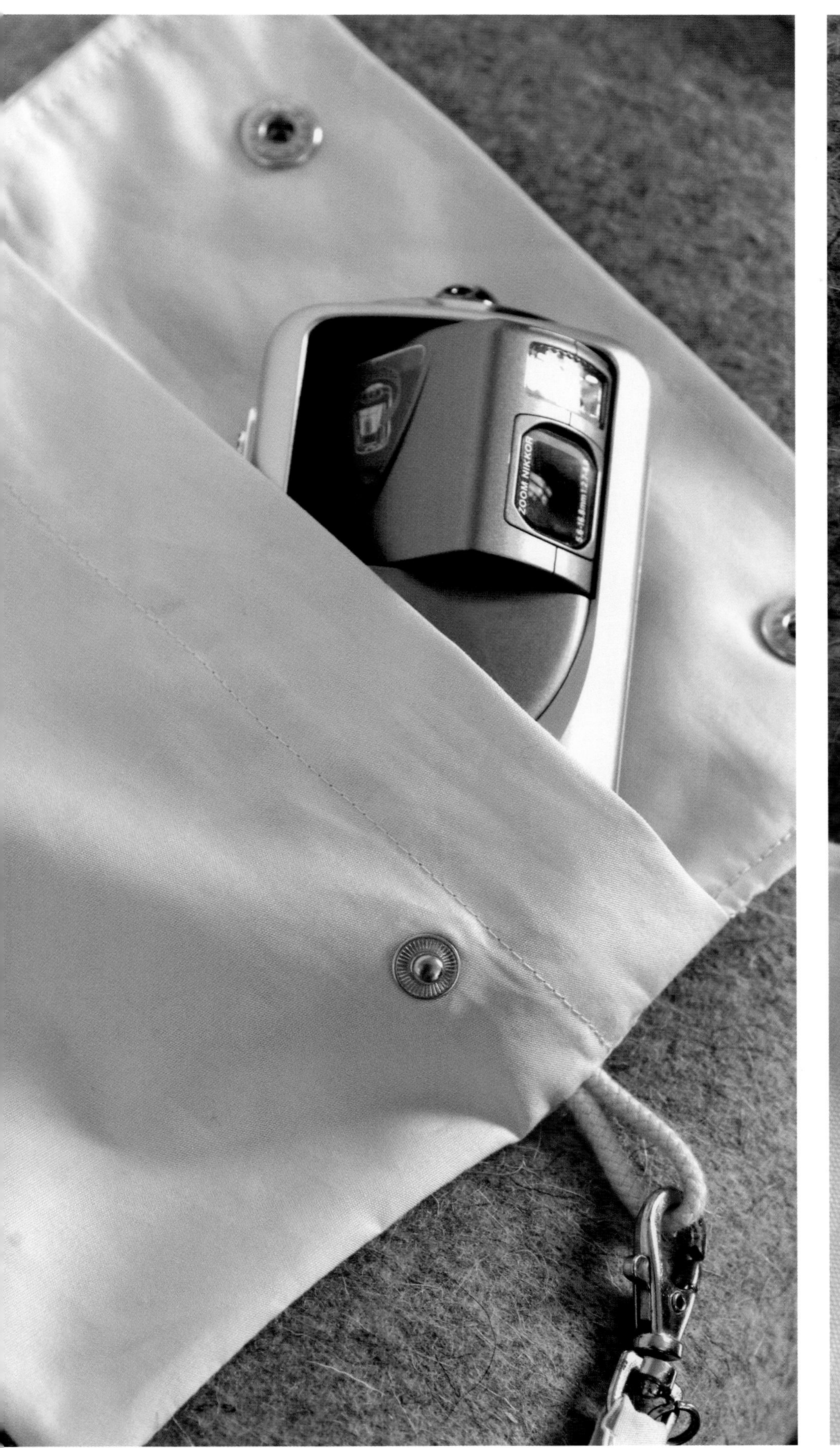
ZOOM NIKKOR

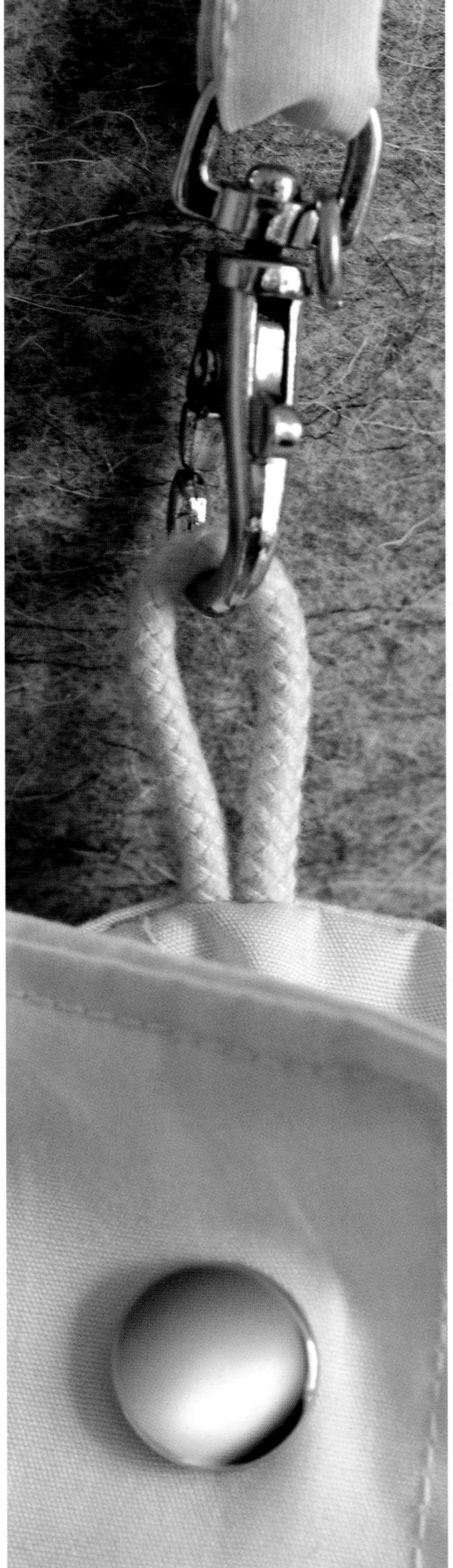

3 With the wrong side out, fold the drawstring insert in half, aligning the short edges. Sew the short edges together using 1/2" (1 cm) seam allowance; leave 2 1/2" (6 cm) unsewn at one end (the top). Press the seam allowances open, fold back and press the allowances at the open end of the seam. Press under the edge of each allowance, then sew through all layers on each side of the seam. (see fig. 21, page 17).

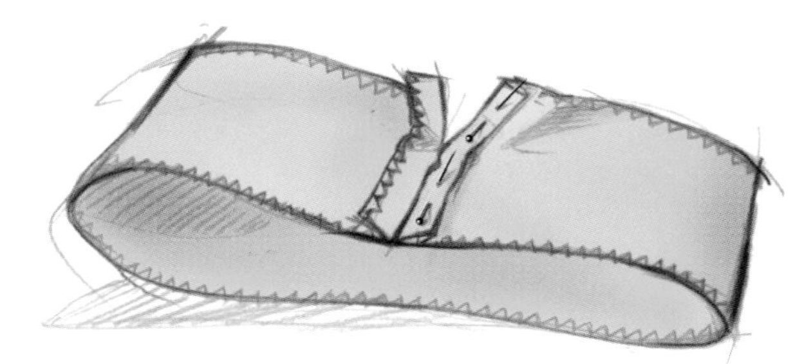

4 To make a casing for the drawstring, fold and press 3/8" (1 cm) and then 1" (2 cm) to the wrong side along the top edge. Pin and then stitch through all layers close to the first fold. Turn the insert right side out.

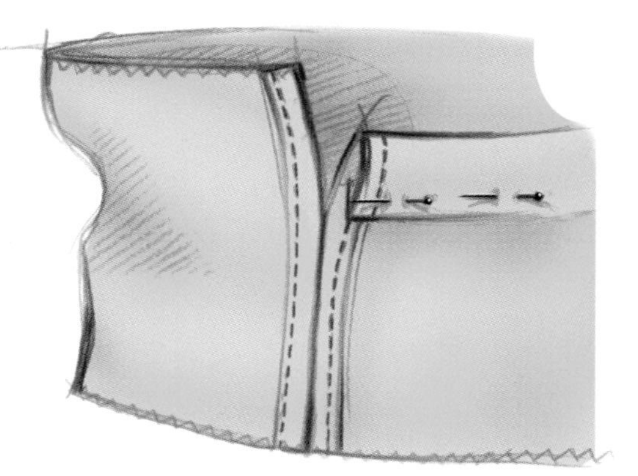

5 Put the insert into the felt bag, aligning the vertical seams and placing the bottom of the insert about 1/2" (1 cm) below the lowest part of the top of the felt. Pin and then sew the insert to the felt by hand; use regular sewing thread and slide your stitches only partway through the felt so they don't show on the outside.

6 Thread the longer piece of cord through the casing; use a safety pin to guide it. Apply glue to one side of each heart cutout; let dry 1 hour; apply a second coat of glue and let dry 20 minutes. Press the hearts together in pairs, inserting one end of the cord at the notch of each. Put them under a heavy object to dry completely.

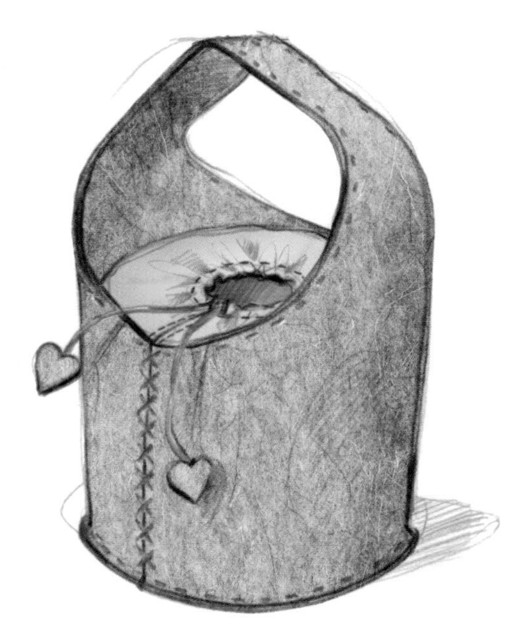

7 On each edge of the strap for the snap hook, fold and press 3/8" (1 cm) to the wrong side. With the right side out, fold the strap in half lengthwise, aligning the long edges. Pin and then sew the open edges together, stitching close to the edge.

8 Insert one end of the strap through the ring of the snap hook. Fold back 1 1/4" (3 cm) and sew the end to itself securely, enclosing the metal bar. Sew the other end of the strap inside the bag at the base of the drawstring insert, using small, strong stitches. Fasten the clip to the loop on the detachable pocket.

Tools

Sewing essentials (see page 7)

Fabric chalk marker,
Tissue paper,
Household scissors,
Zipper foot for your sewing machine,
Gripper-snap setting tool.

Materials

- Black cotton brushed twill: 35" x 24" (84 cm x 60 cm)
- Black chintz (for the lining): 35" x 24" (84 cm x 60 cm)
- Batting: 33" x 23" (80 cm x 58 cm)
- Black zipper, 6" (15 cm) long
- Black cord, 1/4" (5 mm) in diameter: 10" (24 cm) length;
- Narrow, flat, black shoelace: 14" (35 cm) length
- 4 rings 1" (2.5 cm) in diameter; 3 key rings 1/2" (1.5 cm) in diameter
- 2 gripper snaps, 1/2" (1.3 cm) in diameter
- 1 snap hook
- Black thread; Spray fabric adhesive

Be sure you have access to a photocopier for enlarging the pattern.

Little black tote-plus

Tote dimensions: 9″ (21.5 cm) wide x 4 1/2″ (11.5 cm) deep x 9″ (23 cm) high (excluding the handles)
Detachable pocket dimensions: 6″ (15 cm) wide x 9″ (22 cm) high
Cell phone case dimensions: 2 1/2″ (6.5 cm) wide x 1″ (2 cm) deep x 5″ (12 cm) high

Prepare the pieces

Photocopy the pattern on page 152, enlarging it to 133%. *Turn to page 152 to see how to arrange the pieces on your fabric.*

Both twill and chintz - Mark and then cut *for the bag:*
2 main pieces 14 1/2" x 10" (35 cm x 25 cm);
1 bottom, adding 1/2" (1 cm) all around;
2 closure flaps 1 1/2" x 2" (3.5 cm x 4.5 cm);
2 handles 3" x 24" (7 cm x 60 cm).
For the detachable pocket:
2 pieces 7" x 10" (17 cm x 24 cm).
For the cell phone case:
1 main piece 3 1/2" x 13" (8.5 cm x 32 cm);
2 gussets 1 1/2" x 5" (4 cm x 11.5 cm).

Chintz only - Mark and then cut *for the bag:*
1 inside ring link 1 1/4" x 3 1/2" (3 cm x 9 cm)
For the detachable pocket:
1 snap hook link 1 1/4" x 2" (3 cm x 5 cm).
Serge or zigzag the edges of each piece.

Batting - Mark and then cut *for the bag:*
2 main pieces 14 1/2" x 10" (35 cm x 25 cm);
1 bottom, adding 1/2" (1 cm) all around;
2 handles 2" x 23" (5 cm x 58 cm).
For the detachable pocket:
1 piece 7" x 10" (17 cm x 24 cm);
For the cell phone case: 1 piece 3 1/2" x 13" (8.5 cm x 32 cm).

Cord - Cut into four 2 1/2" (6 cm) lengths.

Tote

1 Spray adhesive on one side of all of batting pieces except the handles. Affix each sprayed piece to the wrong side of a corresponding piece of cotton twill, aligning the edges; press each with your hand to adhere the layers. On each, mark the midpoint of each edge. As shown in the drawing below, baste between opposite marks; also baste diagonally from corner to corner (baste the bottom piece too).

2 On the right side of each piece, mark chalk lines parallel to each diagonal basting line, spacing the lines 1¼" (3 cm) apart. Sew through both layers on each of the drawn and basted diagonal lines.

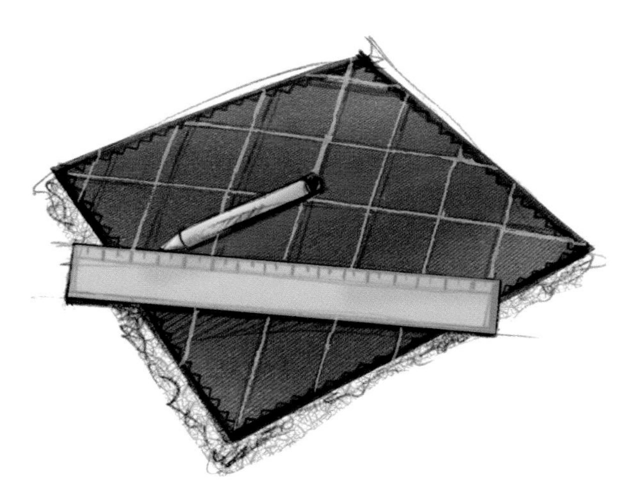

3 Place the two quilted main pieces right sides together. Pin them together along the shorter edges (the side seams), then sew, using ½" (1 cm) seam allowance. Press the seam allowances open.

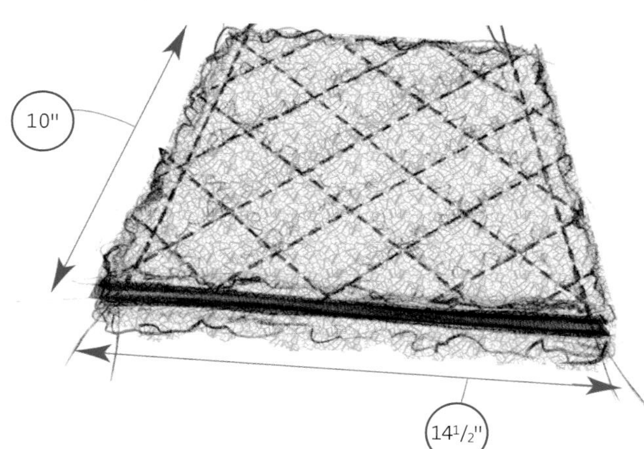

4 On the wrong side of the quilted bottom, mark the midpoint of each end (indicated by the black triangles on the pattern). With the right sides together, pin one open end of the tube made in step 3 to the bottom, aligning the side seams with the marks on the bottom. Baste and then sew, using ½" (1 cm) seam allowance.

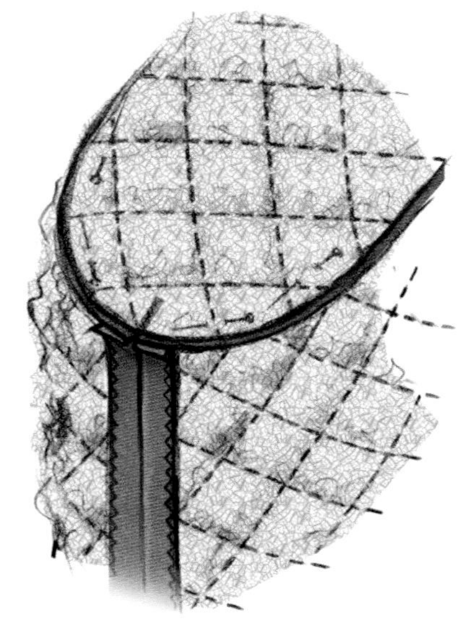

Notch the seam allowances along the curves; then press them open. Fold and press ½" (1 cm) to the wrong side along the top edge of the bag, .

5 On the chintz link strip, fold and press 1/4" (5 mm) to the wrong side. With the right side out, fold the strip in half lengthwise. Pin the long open edges closed; then stitch close to the edge. Insert the strip through one of the smaller (key) rings, bringing the ends together to enclose the metal ring. Topstitch the edges closed, pivoting across near the ring.

6 Place one of the chintz main pieces right side up. Lay the ring link on it, placing the link on one of the shorter edges about 3" (8 cm) from one of the longer edges (the top) and aligning the strip end with the edge of the fabric (so the ring is on top of the fabric). Place the second chintz main piece right-side down on top of the first, aligning the edges. Follow steps 3 and 4 to sew the main pieces together and then to the chintz bottom.

7 With the right sides together, pin each twill closure flap to a corresponding piece of chintz. Sew each pair along both long edges and across one end, using 1/4" (5 mm) seam allowance. Trim the seam allowance at the corners. Turn the closure flaps right side out; press. Affix a gripper snap to the flaps, centering each piece of the snap 5/8" (1.5 cm) from the seamed end (see page 11); make sure the twill side of both flaps faces in the same direction when the snap is closed.

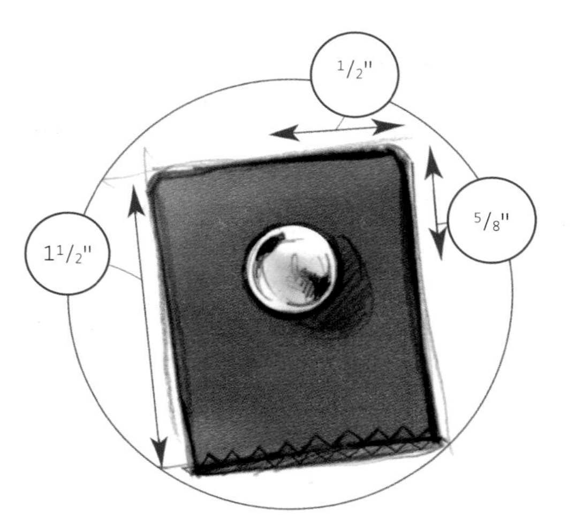

8 Insert a piece of cord through each of the larger metal rings; bring the ends of each piece of cord together to enclose the ring and secure them with a few small hand stitches.

9 Make sure the quilted bag is right side out and the chintz bag wrong side out. Insert the chintz bag into the quilted bag, aligning the seams and top edges. As shown below, insert the cord-and-ring assemblies between the layers on the top edge, placing one assembly 3" (7.5 cm) on each side of each side seam. Snap the closure flaps closed; insert one end in the center of the top on one side and the other end opposite it on the other side; unsnap. Pin the bags together along the top; sew close to the edge.

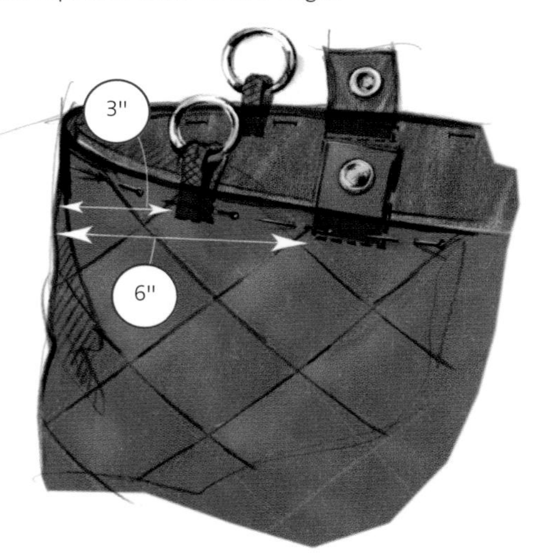

10 With the right sides together, pin each twill handle to a corresponding chintz handle. Sew each pair along all edges using 1/2" (1 cm) seam allowance; leave an 8" (20 cm) long opening in one long edge. Trim the seam allowance at each corner. Fold back the seam allowance along each opening and press it. Turn each handle right side out. Using the eraser end of a pencil, slide the batting (the pieces cut for this purpose) inside each handle. Slipstitch the openings closed (see fig. 16, page 16). Referring to the photographs, knot the ends of the handles through the rings at the top of the bag.

Detachable pocket

1 As you did for the tote, diagonally quilt one piece of twill with the corresponding piece of batting. Align it, right sides together, on top of the corresponding piece of chintz. Pin and sew along both long edges and across one end using 1/2" (1 cm) seam allowance. Diagonally trim the seam allowance at the corners; also trim the batting out of the seam allowance all around. Turn the piece right side out.

2 At the open end of the piece just made, turn in 1/2" (1 cm) along each layer; press and then baste closed. Pin this edge to one side of the zipper tape, leaving the teeth exposed (see fig. 7, page 12). Baste, and then, using the zipper foot,

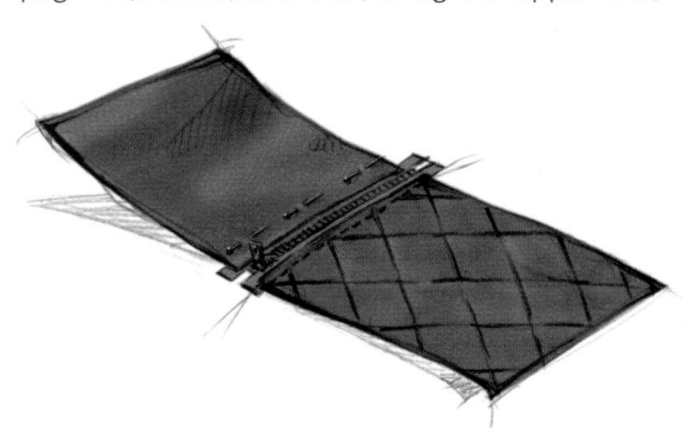

sew about 1/8" (3 mm) from the edge of the fabric. On each edge of the remaining piece of twill, fold and press 1/2" (1 cm) to the wrong side. Referring to the drawing above, place it on the zipper tape, leaving the teeth exposed. Pin; sew together.

3 Working as for step 5 of the tote, sew the chintz link for the snap hook. Insert the link through the eye of the snap hook; fold to bring the ends together; baste.

4 With the right side out, fold the piece with the zipper in half along the zipper, aligning the edges. Pin along the open edges. Then insert the end of the snap hook link made in step 3 on one of the long sides, about 1 1/2" (4 cm) from the zipper. Tuck the ends of the zipper tape into the

inside of the pocket. Baste the edges of the pocket closed, then beginning at the zipper on one side, sew all around close to the edge; stop when you reach the zipper again. Thread a small key ring onto the eye of the zipper pull.

Cell phone case

1 As you did for the tote, diagonally quilt the larger piece of twill with the corresponding piece of batting. Align it, right sides together, on top of the corresponding piece of chintz. Pin and sew along both long edges and across one end, using ½" (1 cm) seam allowance. Diagonally trim the seam allowance at the corners; also trim the batting out of the seam allowance all around.

2 Turn the piece right side out. At the open end, turn in ½" (1 cm) along each layer; press and then baste closed. Sew through all layers close to the basted edge.

3 On each edge of the twill gussets and of the chintz gussets, fold and press ½" (1 cm) to the wrong side. With the wrong sides together, align each twill gusset on a chintz gusset. Pin and then sew all around each, close to the edges.

4 On the twill face of the quilted piece, mark each long edge 4½" (11.5 cm) from the end stitched in step 2. Mark the midpoint of one end of each gusset. With the chintz sides together and aligning the marks, pin the end of each gusset to the quilted piece. Then, working out from the midpoint to the top of the gusset in each direction, pin each gusset to the quilted piece. Referring to the photo on page 107, fold the shoelace in half, insert the folded end through the remaining small key ring and pass the ends of the lace through the fold; pull to secure the ring. Insert the ends of the lace between the gusset and back of the case as shown. Slipstitch the gusset to the quilted piece (see fig. 16, page 16).

5 Affix the female portion of the gripper snap to the flap of the case, centering it about ¾" (2 cm) from the end. Affix the male portion of the snap to the top of the case front, centering it about ½" (1 cm) below the edge.

Tips

To easily space the quilting lines, use a 1¼" wide ruler or a transparent gridded ruler as a guide.

To turn the handles right side out, use the eraser end of a pencil to push the fabric from each end to the opening in the side. Use the fingers of one hand to ease the fabric over the pencil while you push with your other hand.

Here's a technique to make it easier to quilt the fabric layered with batting by machine—it will help the pieces move smoothly and keep the feed dogs from catching on the rough material: Place your work, batting side down, on a piece of tissue paper or an interfacing specifically formulated to facilitate this kind of work; sew through all layers. When you've finished the quilting, tear off the tissue or interfacing.

Prepare the pieces

Photocopy the two patterns on pages 153 and 154, enlarging the main piece to 215% and copying the cell phone case in the size shown. *Turn to page 153 to see how to position the pieces on your fabric.*

Rubber - Mark and then cut:
1 wrapper 13" x 26" (33 cm x 66 cm);
1 strap 1 3/8" x 33" (3.5 cm x 84 cm);
2 magnet pockets 1 1/2" x 1 1/2" (4 cm x 4 cm).

Felt - Mark and then cut:
2 main pieces;
2 handle links 1 1/4" x 2 3/8" (3 cm x 6 cm);
2 straps 1 3/8" x 17" (3.5 cm x 43 cm);
1 cell phone case;
2 case flaps 2 3/8" x 6 1/4" (6 cm x 16 cm).

1 Insert a handle link through one of the eyes on each double swivel ring. Fold each link in half, bringing the ends together to enclose the ring. Lay one of the felt main pieces on your work surface. Place an assembled ring/handle link on each long edge, 12 1/4" (31 cm) from the narrower end (which will be the bottom of the bag); be sure each ring lies on the main piece and the end of each link is even with the edge. Lay the other main piece on top, aligning all the edges; pin. Sew along both long edges and across the bottom, using 1/2" (1 cm) seam allowance. Sew again through each link to reinforce it. Diagonally trim the seam allowance at each bottom corner.

City bag

Bag dimensions: 10 1/4" (26 cm) wide x 1 3/4" (5 cm) deep x 11 1/2" (29 cm) high (excluding the handles)
Cell phone case dimensions: 1 3/4" (4.5 cm) wide x 1 1/8" (3 cm) deep x 5" (13 cm) high

Tools

Sewing essentials (see page 7),
Tissue paper,
Ballpoint pen,
Felt-tip marker with nonpermanent ink,
Household scissors.

Materials

- Yellow rubber anti-skid rug matting: 14 3/8" x 33" (36.5 cm x 84 cm)
- Purple industrial felt, 1/8" (2-3 mm) thick: 35" x 19 3/4" (88 cm x 50 cm)
- 2 double swivel rings, about 3/4" (2 cm) in diameter (from a hardware store)
- 1 sew-on snap, about 1/2" (1.5 cm) in diameter
- 2 magnets, about 1/2" (1.5 cm) in diameter
- Thread: Purple, yellow

Be sure you have access to a photocopier for enlarging the pattern.

2 To box each bottom corner of the bag, align the side seam on the bottom seam, forming a triangle 1¾" (4.5 cm) wide at the base. Sew through all layers at the base of each triangle and fold the triangles onto the bottom of the bag.

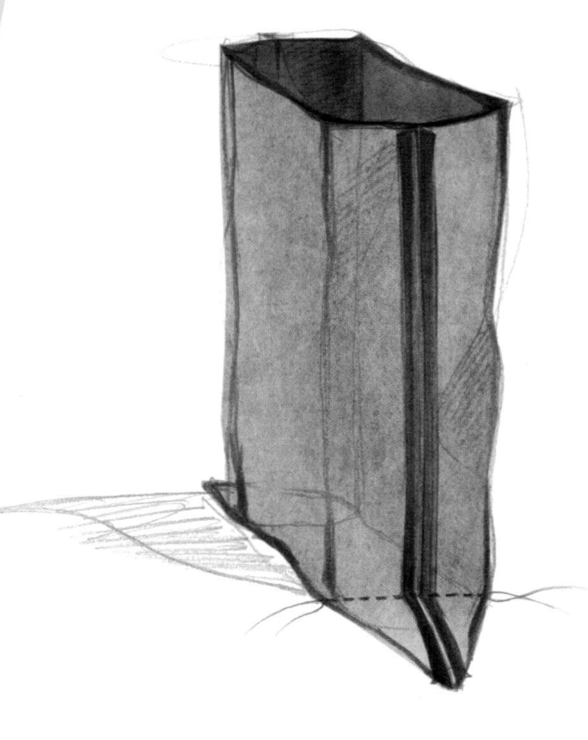

3 Fold the rubber wrapper in half, aligning the short edges; the fold is the bottom of the bag. Pin and then sew along each side edge using ½" (1 cm) seam allowance (sandwich with tissue paper for easier sewing). Open the seam allowances with your fingers. Box the corners as in step 2. Turn the wrapper right side out.

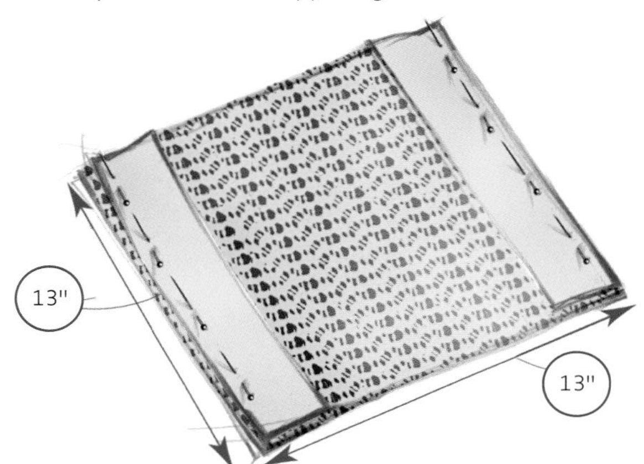

4 Place the flaps for the cell phone case one on top of the other. Pin; then sew all around close to the edges. To form the bottom of the cell phone case, fold the felt so that edges A and A′ align; sew, using ¼" (5 mm) seam allowance; begin a short distance from the diagonal fold and stop stitching at the notch shown in the drawing below. Repeat to sew edges B and B′. Turn the case right side out. Crease along fold 1; clip the allowance at the bottom corner; stitch close to the fold. Repeat along fold 2.

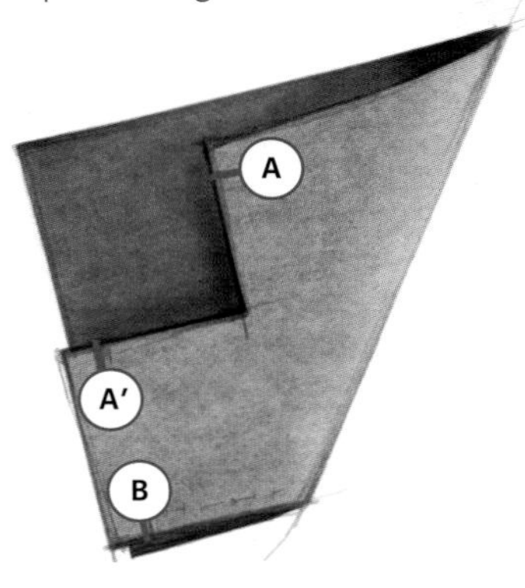

5 Center the flap over one of the vertical seams on the wrapper, placing the bottom of the flap 5" (13.5 cm) above the wrapper bottom; pin. Pin the phone case on top of the flap, placing the case bottom 2½" (6.5 cm) above the wrapper bottom. Stitch the case to the wrapper.

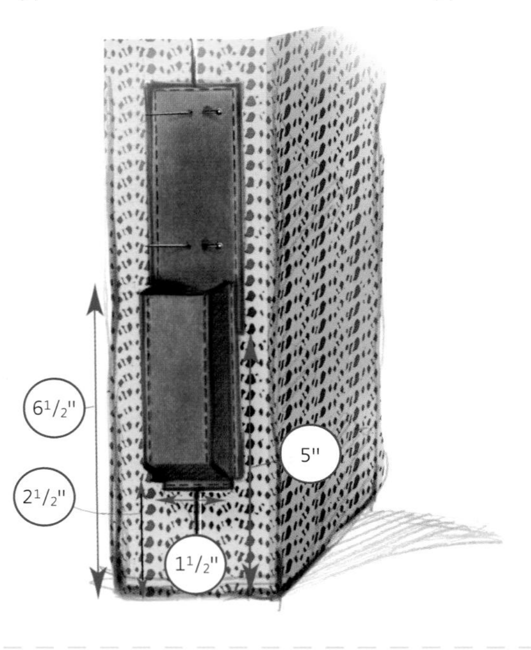

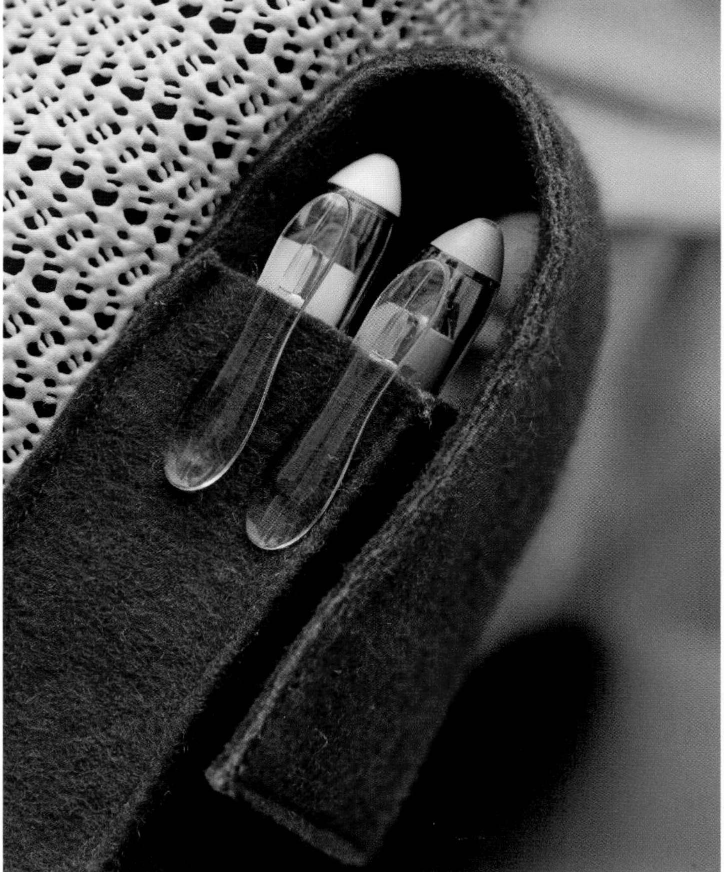

6 Sew the female portion of the snap to the face of the phone case, centering it 1" (2.5 cm) below the open edge. Sew the male portion of the snap to the inside of the flap, centering it 1¼" (3 cm) from the end of the flap.

7 Place the magnet pockets on the inside of the wrapper, centering one on each side at the top edge; pin. Sew each pocket along the sides and across the bottom, using straight hand stiches (see fig. 14, page 16). Slide a magnet into each pocket; baste the top of the pocket closed.

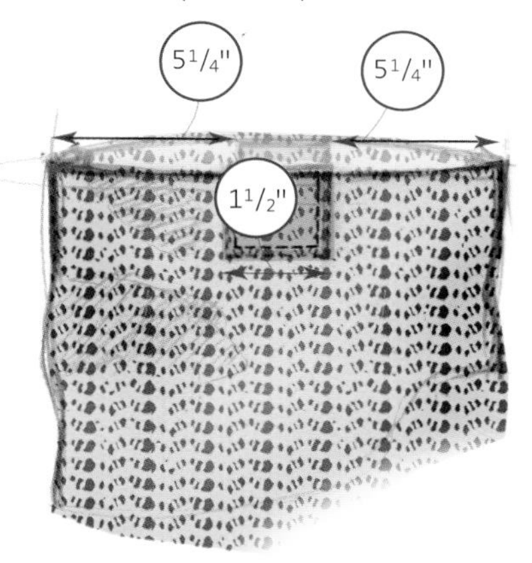

8 Make sure the felt lining is wrong side out. Insert it in the wrapper, aligning the vertical seams and the bottoms. Pin the felt to the rubber and then sew around the top of the bag just below the top of the wrapper. To form the cuff, fold the extending felt in half; then fold the two layers down together over the rubber.

9 Sew the two felt straps together at one end, using 1/2" (1 cm) seam allowance. Open the seam allowances and topstitch through both layers on each side of the seam. Place the felt strap wrong side down on the rubber strap. Pin them together along the edges. Cut each end of the strap into a point as shown below and in the photos. Sew all around through all thicknesses, stitching close to the edge.

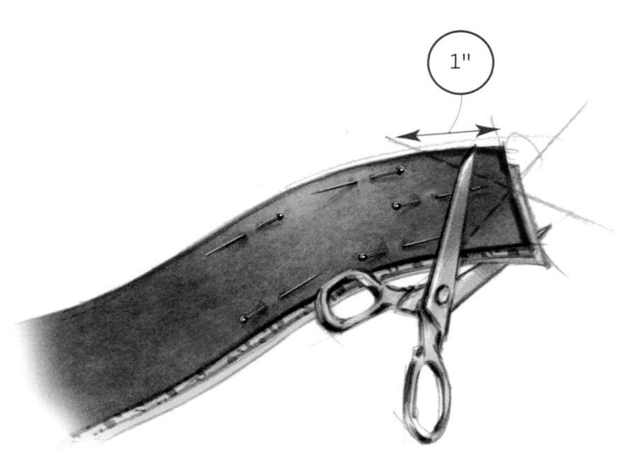

10 Insert each end of the strap through one of the swivel rings. Fold it back so the purple point lies on the rubber and the ring is enclosed, as shown below; pin and sew along the edges of the point and across the strap.

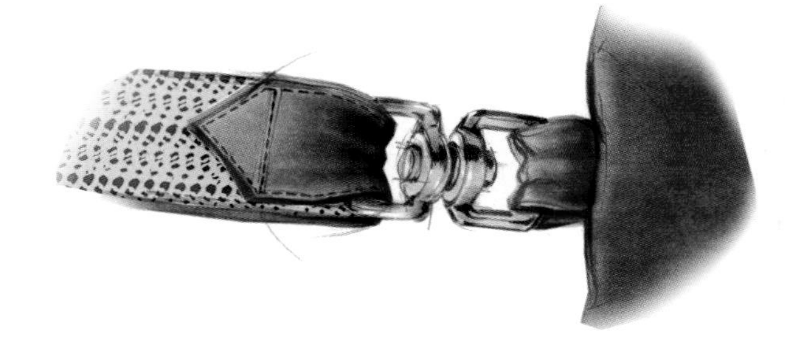

Tips

Pin through the rubber in such a way that your stitches will fall in the holes left by the pins–place the pins parallel to the edge and pull them out as you sew.

The sewing machine presser foot will easily catch in the molded rubber material used for this bag, and the feed dog teeth will snag it. To avoid damaging the rubber, sandwich your work between pieces of tissue paper, aligning the paper edges with the edges of the rubber. Sew through all layers; then, when the seam is complete, tear off the tissue paper.

To sew the strap, put purple thread in the needle and yellow thread in the bobbin. Then sew with the rubber on the bottom. Switch to purple in the bobbin too when you sew the points to secure the swivel rings.

MOTOROLA

Tools

Sewing essentials (see page 7), Felt-tip marker with nonpermanent ink, Household scissors, Zipper foot for your sewing machine.

Materials

- Aqua glazed rainwear fabric: 43½" x 39½" (110 cm x 100 cm)
- Khaki plastic sports-weight zipper, 21½" (55 cm) long
- Self-adhesive Velcro, 1" (2.5 cm) wide: 24" (61 cm) long
- 2 metal rings, ¾" (2 cm) in diameter
- 1 snap hook
- Aqua thread
- Adhesive tape or removable masking tape
- Contact cement or sturdy craft glue

Be sure you have access to a photocopier for enlarging the patterns.

Aqua backpack

Bag dimensions: 11" (28 cm) wide x 2" (5 cm) deep x 13¾" (35 cm) high (excluding the straps)
Detachable pocket dimensions: 4½" (11.5 cm) wide x 6" (15 cm) high
Cell phone case dimensions: 2" (5 cm) wide x ⅜" (1 cm) deep x 4⅜" (11 cm) high

Prepare the pieces

Photocopy the five patterns on pages 155 through 157; enlarge the main piece to 156%; enlarge the top strap to 363% and the side strap to 171%; enlarge the applied pocket to 200%; enlarge the cell phone case to 173%.
Turn to page 155 to see how to arrange the pieces on your fabric. Be sure to reverse the patterns as shown to complete the main piece; also reverse (turn over) the strap patterns to make a mirrored pair of each.
Mark and then cut:
For the backpack: 2 main pieces;
2 top straps; 2 side straps;
2 top (zipper) gussets 1¼" x 22½" (3 cm x 57 cm);
1 bottom gusset 2¾" x 28" (7 cm x 70 cm).
For the applied pocket:
1 pocket; 1 flap 7¾" x 15½" (19.5 cm x 39 cm);
2 ring links ⅜" x 3¼" (1 cm x 8 cm).
For the detachable pocket:
1 pocket 7" x 10" (17 cm x 25 cm);
1 closure flap 1⅝" x 9½" (4 cm x 24 cm).
For the cell phone case: 1 case;
1 snap hook strap ⅝" x 10" (1.5 cm x 26 cm);
2 ring links ⅜" x 3½" (1 cm x 9 cm).
On the wrong side of both main pieces, mark the center of the top edge (the black triangle on the pattern; on the right side of one of them, mark the placement for the straps (the black diamonds on the pattern). Mark the midpoint of both long edges on the wrong side of both top gussets.

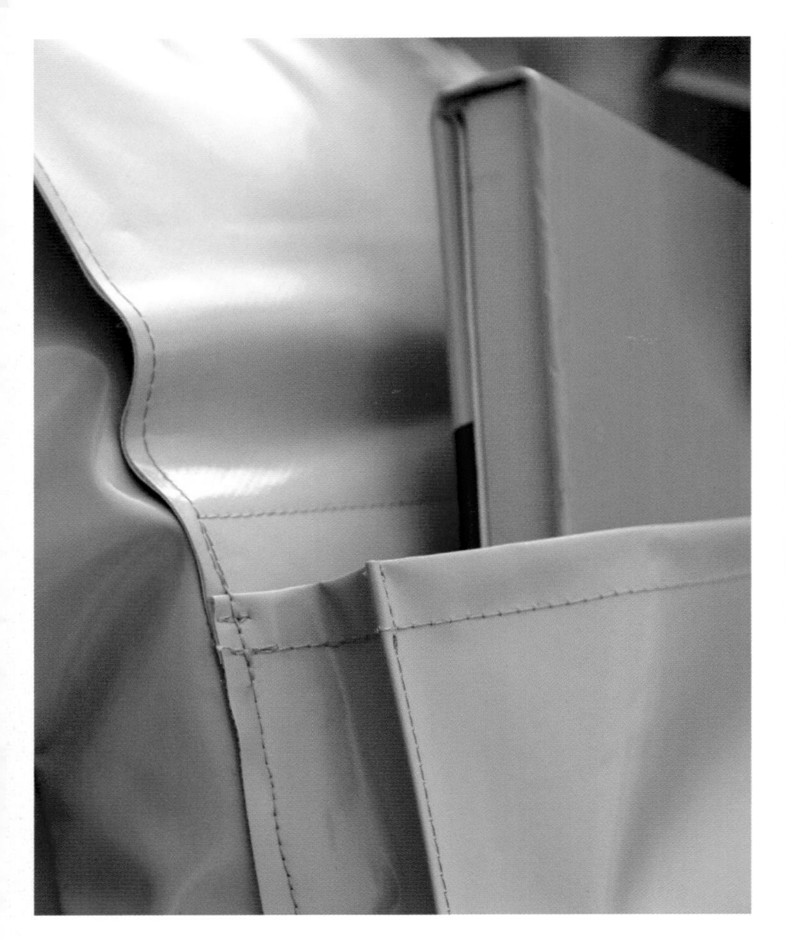

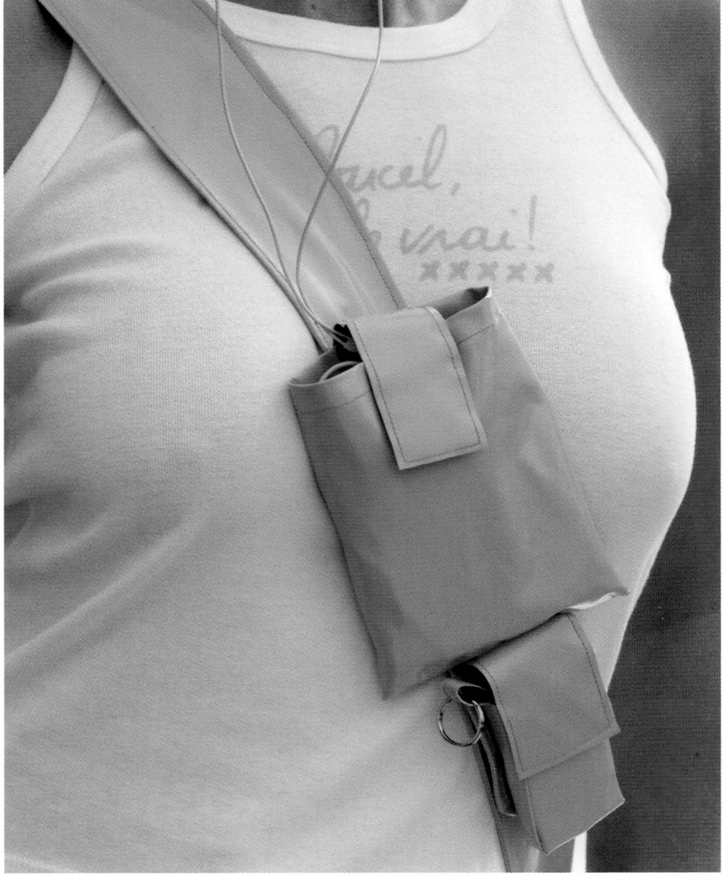

Backpack

1 Fold the flap of the applied pocket in half, right side out, aligning the short edges. Topstitch along both long edges and across the fold, stitching $1/4$" (5 mm) from the edge. Cut the fabric to round the corners at the fold.

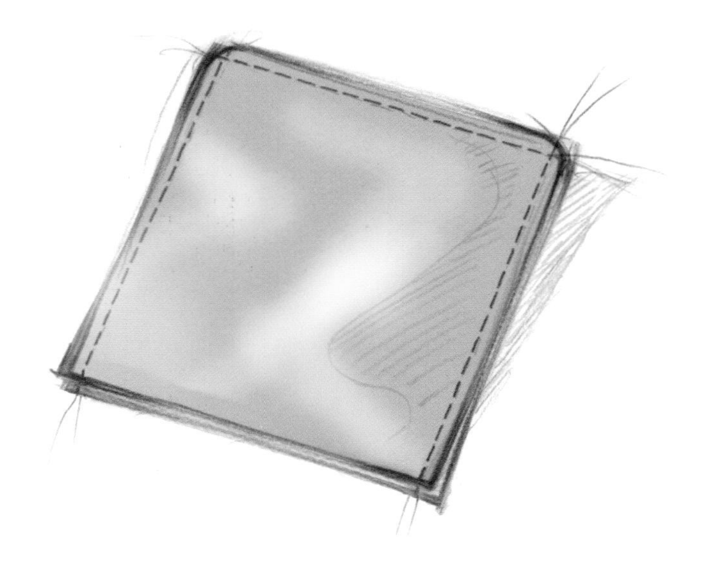

2 Fold the longest edge of the pocket (gray margin on the pattern) to the wrong side. Sew close to the cut edge. To form the bottom of the pocket, fold the fabric, right side out, so that edges A and A′ align; sew, using 1/8" (2 mm) seam allowance and stopping 1/8" (2 mm) from the open edge. Repeat to sew edges B and B′. Referring to the pattern, crease the pocket, right side out, along the side folds and stitch close to each crease. In the same way, crease and stitch the bottom fold.

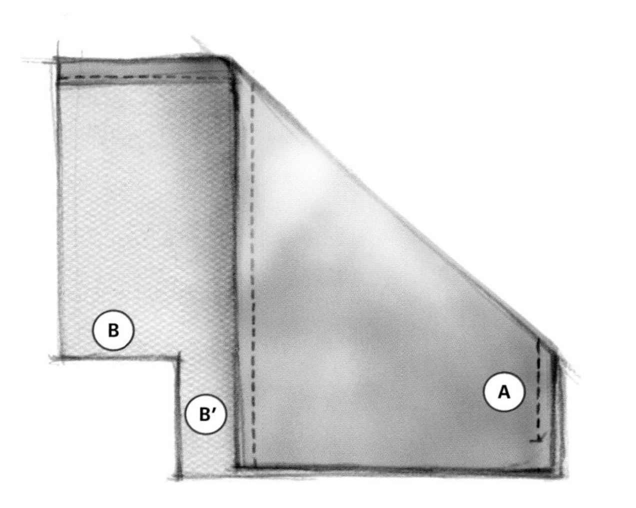

3 Fold the ring link in half, right side out, bringing the ends together. Topstitch both long edges, stitching close to the edge. Insert the link through one of the metal rings; bring the ends together to enclose the ring.

4 Place the main piece that is marked only at the top center right side up. Center the pocket flap on it, aligning the folded edge of the flap with the top of the main piece. Pin and then sew the open edge of the flap to the bag, stitching 2" (5 cm) from the edge. On one edge of the flap, insert the ring link just below the bottom stitching as shown in the drawing below. Center the folded pocket on the main piece, aligning the upper edge 5/8" (1.5 cm) below the seam at the bottom of the flap as shown. Pin and then sew through all layers along the side and bottom edges of the pocket, securing the ring link.

5 Cut a 6 1/2" (17 cm) piece of Velcro; separate the halves. Affix the prickly half to the center of the pocket, 2 3/4" (7 cm) below the top edge. Affix the soft half to the inside of the flap, centering it 5/8" (1.5 cm) from the folded edge.

6 Place the zipper right side up. Align a top gusset strip, right side up, on each side of the zipper teeth; arrange the whole so the gussets extend equally at both ends and the total width is 2¾" (7 cm); pin each strip in place. Using the zipper foot, sew each gusset strip to the zipper tape (see fig. 7, page 11).

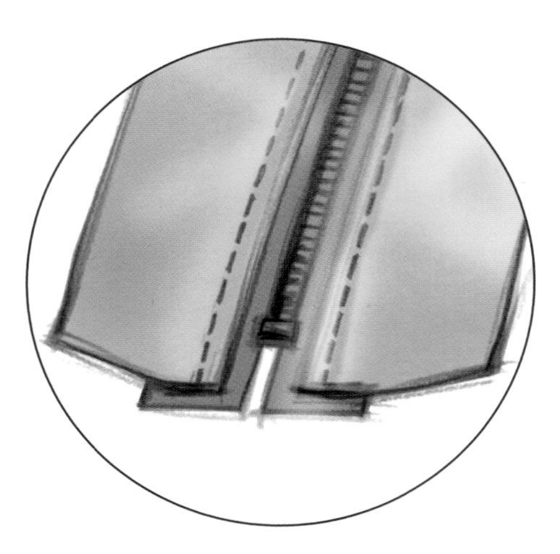

7 At the ends of the bottom gusset, fold ½" (1 cm) to the wrong side and crease with your finger. Lap the folded ends over the ends of the top gusset, covering the ends of the zipper tape; affix with adhesive tape. Place the ring thus made around one of the main pieces and check to see that it fits (allow ⅜" [1 cm] seam allowance). If needed, refold the ends of the bottom gusset until the ring fits. When you are satisfied, remove the tape and topstitch the bottom gusset to the top gussets, stitching close to the folded edge at each end of the bottom gusset.

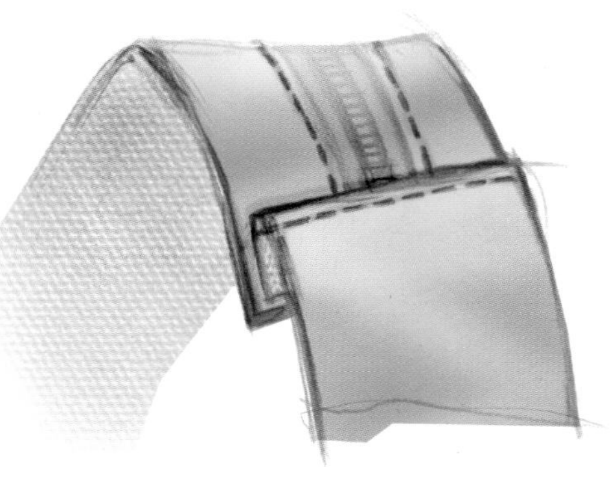

8 With the right sides together, pin the gusset to the perimeter of the main piece that has the pocket; align the top center marks and the edges. Pin and then sew, using ⅜" (1 cm) seam allowance.

9 With the right sides together, place the top straps one on top of the other. Pin and then sew, using ⅜" (1 cm) seam allowance; leave the flat end open. Notch the allowances along the curves. Turn the strap right side out and topstitch close to the edge. Cut two 8½" (22 cm) lengths of Velcro and separate the halves. Affix a soft half to each face of the strap, placing one end of the Velcro near the rounded end of the strap and centering it between the side edges.

10 Follow step 9 to sew the side strap. Lay it with the deeper curved edge on top and the wide end to your right. Affix a prickly piece of the Velcro cut in step 9 to the face now up, positioning the Velcro as you did in step 9.

11 Fold the snap hook strap in half, right side out, bringing the ends together. Pin the long edges closed; topstitch close to the edge. Insert the strap through the ring of the snap hook. Apply glue across one end, covering ⅜" (1 cm); leave a 1⅜" (3.5 cm) space and then apply another ⅜" (1 cm) band of glue. Let the glue dry for 20 minutes. Position the ring between the two glued areas and then fold the strap to align them, enclosing the ring; press firmly with your fingers to adhere the glue.

12 Place the top and side straps on the remaining main piece, aligning their open ends with the edge of the main piece between the corresponding marks (as shown below). Insert the free end of the snap hook strap into the open end of the top strap as shown. Open the zipper so you'll be able to turn the bag

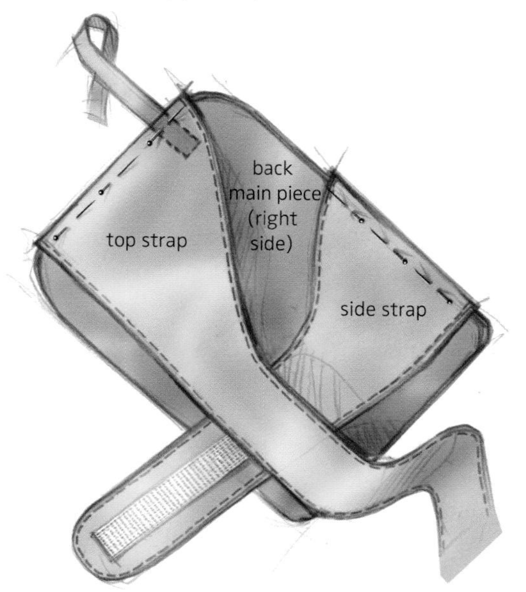

right side out later; then, with the right sides together, align the free edge of the gusset with the perimeter of the second main piece (be sure to align the top center marks). Pin and then sew, using 3/8" (1 cm) seam allowance. Turn the bag right side out.

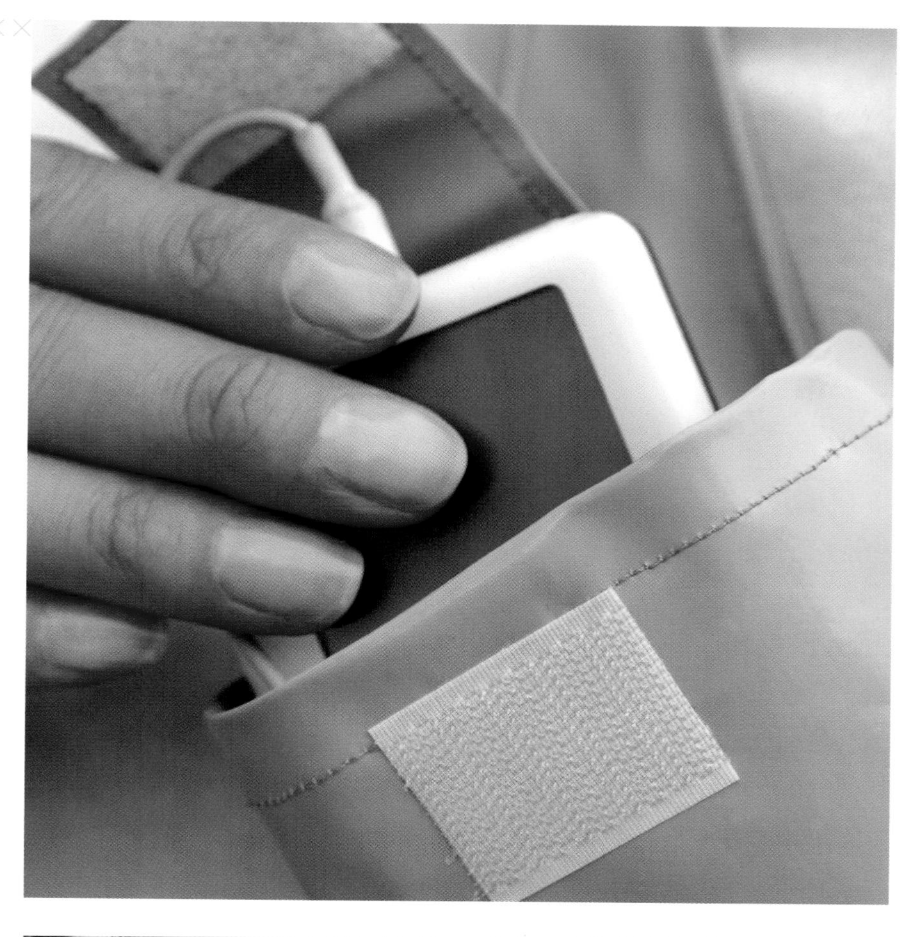

Detachable pocket

1 With the wrong side out, fold the detachable pocket in half, aligning the short edges. Pin and then sew the short edges together using 1/2" (1 cm) seam allowance. Using your finger, press the seam allowance open. Adjust the tube so the seam falls in the center of the opposite side. At one end (the bottom) sew the layers together using 1/2" (1 cm) seam allowance. Diagonally trim the corner allowances. At the opposite end (the top) fold 1/2" (1 cm) to the wrong side; stitch close to the cut edge. Turn the pocket right side out.

2 With the right side out, fold the closure flap in half, bringing the short edges together. Stitch all around, close to the edge. On the back of the pocket, mark a space for the end of the flap 1 1/4" (3 cm) below the edge and centered over the seam. Apply glue inside the marked area and also to the corresponding area on the flap. Let dry 20 minutes; then assemble so that the flap extends above the top of the pocket.

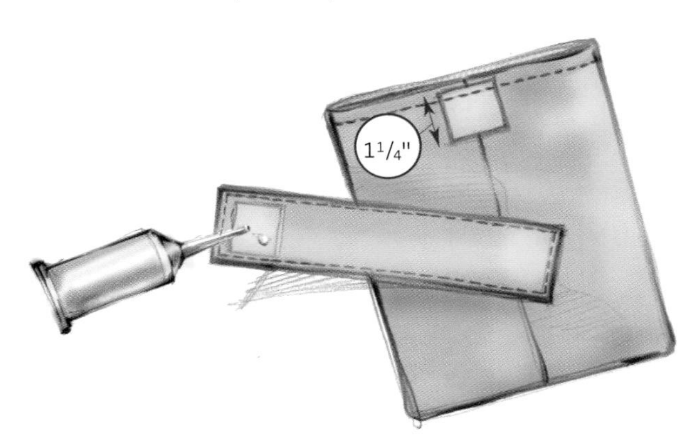

3 Cut a 1 1/4" (3 cm) length of Velcro. Affix its prickly half horizontally across the front of the pocket, just below the line of stitches. Affix the soft half to the inside of closure flap, leaving a small border at the end of the flap. Cut a 4 3/4" (12 cm) length of Velcro and affix the prickly half to the back of the pocket, centering it top to bottom over the seam. Reserve the soft half for another project.

Cell phone case

1 Fold the hem margin shown in gray on the pattern 3/8" (1 cm) to the wrong side; sew close to the cut edge. With the right side out, fold the flap at the opposite end in half as indicated on the pattern. Pin and then sew close to both long edges and across the open end.

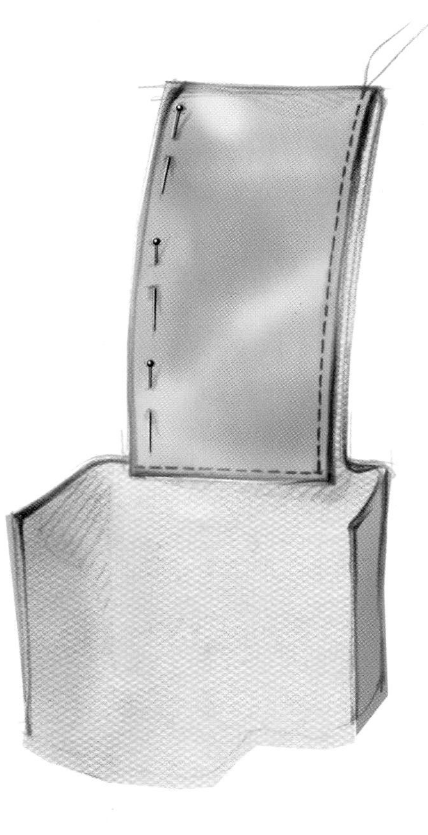

2 To form the bottom of the case, fold the fabric right sides together so that edges A and A′ align; sew, using 1/4" (5 mm) seam allowance. Repeat to sew edges B and B′. Align mark C with C′ and D with D′; pin and then sew each side seam. Turn the case right side out.

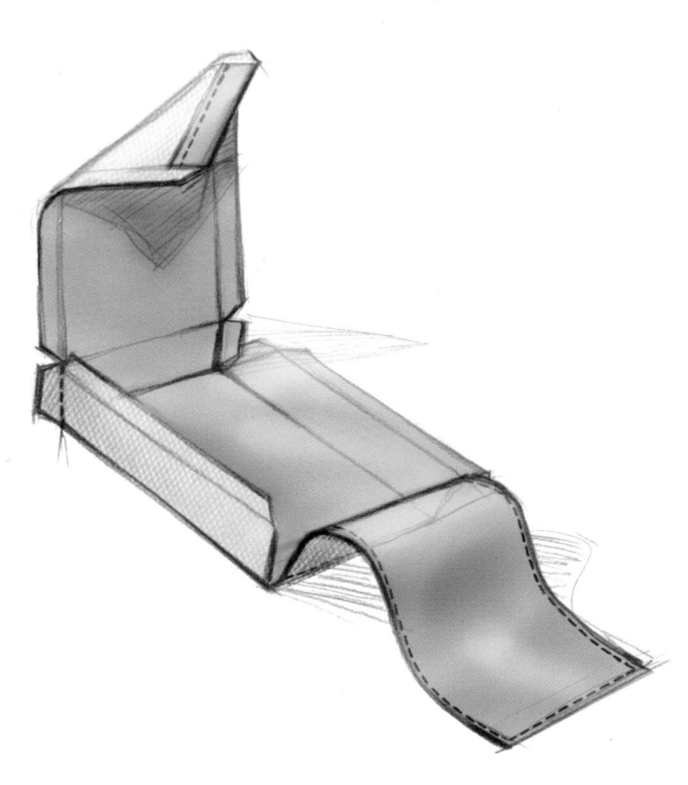

3 Cut a 3/4" (2 cm) piece of Velcro. Affix the prickly half horizontally on the front of the case, just below the top edge. Affix the soft half to the inside of the flap, close to the free end. Cut a 3 1/2" (9 cm) length of Velcro and affix the soft half vertically to the back of the case, centering it just above the bottom.

4 Make a ring link following step 3 of the backpack. On one face of the link, apply a narrow band of glue to both ends. Let the glue dry 20 minutes; then press the ends together; securing the ring. Referring to the top right photo on page 118, glue the doubled end of the link inside one side of the case.

Tips

Many of the seams on this project are are sewn with the fabric wrong sides together so that the edges are exposed. Make sure you choose a fabric that doesn't ravel.

Pins can leave permanent marks in glazed or rubberized fabric. Test-fit the pieces of each component with adhesive or masking tape before you pin them.

Pin the pieces together exactly on the seamlines, with the pins parallel to the edges. Pull out the pins as you sew to prevent them from being caught by the presser foot.

Glazed and rubberized fabrics may not move smoothly through your sewing machine; if they get stuck on the feed dogs they may be damaged. To prevent this, sandwich your work between pieces of tissue paper, aligning the paper edges with the edges of the fabric. Sew through all thicknesses; then, when the seam is complete, tear off the tissue paper.

Prepare the pieces

Photocopy the patterns on pages 158 and 159, enlarging the main piece to 106%, the gussets to 255% and copying the zipper tab and handle end detail at the size shown. *Turn to page 159 to see how to arrange the pieces on your fabric (be sure to fold the fabric as shown).*

Tablecloth pad -Mark and then cut:
2 main pieces;
1 top gusset;
1 bottom 15¾" x 6¾" (40.5 cm x 17 cm);
1 zipper pull;
2 handles 2⅜" x 21" (6 cm x 53 cm);
2 zipper stops.

Cut both ends of each handle using the detail pattern. Using the rotary cutter and following the pattern, slit the center of the gusset (for the zipper). On the right side, mark the midpoint of the top of the main pieces and the gusset ends (indicated by black triangles on the patterns). Also mark the midpoint of each end of the bottom. With nonpermanent ink, mark the placement for the handles on the right and wrong sides of each main piece.

Twill - Mark and then cut:
2 main pieces and 2 top gussets, adding ⅜" (1 cm) seam allowance on all edges except the fold on each;
1 bottom 16¾" x 7½" (43 cm x 19 cm);
1 interior pocket 8" x 5¼" (20 cm x 13 cm);
4 handle reinforcements 3" x 3" (7 cm x 7 cm).

Serge or zigzag the perimeter of each piece. On the wrong side, mark the midpoints of the main piece, gusset ends, and bottom ends as you did for the pieces cut from the pad.

Electric cord: - Cut into 2 equal lengths.

Go bowling

Dimensions: 15″ (39.5 cm) wide x 6¼″ (12 cm) deep x 8″ (21 cm) high (excluding the handles)

Tools

Sewing essentials (see page 7),
Tissue paper,
Felt-tip marker with nonpermanent ink,
Household scissors,
Cutting mat and ruler,
Rotary cutter,
Zipper foot for your sewing machine.

Materials

- Chestnut-color tablecloth pad (for the exterior): 40" x 24½" (103 cm x 62 cm)
- Pink cotton brushed twill (for the lining): 46½" x 28" (102 cm x 71 cm)
- Beige zipper, 22" (55 cm) long
- Electrical cord (for the handles), ¼" (7 mm) in diameter: 33" (84 cm) long
- Thread: Chestnut-color, pink
- Contact cement or strong glue

Be sure you have access to a photocopier for enlarging the patterns.

1 Center a length of elecrical cord on the wrong side of each handle. Wrap the handle around the cord, bringing the long edges together; pin to enclose the cord. Sew through both layers 1/4" (5 mm) from the edge, using the zipper foot; leave the shaped ends open.

2 Pin a handle reinforcement to the wrong side of each exterior main piece where marked; baste in place. Curve a handle over the right side of each main piece and pin the ends where marked. Sew through all layers close to the edge of each handle end.

3 Place the exterior top gusset wrong side up. Lay the closed zipper wrong side down on top, centered over the slit. Pin the zipper tape to the gusset; baste. Using the zipper foot and working with the gusset on top, sew parallel to and a short distance from the slit edge, pivoting across the zipper ends (see fig. 7, page 12).

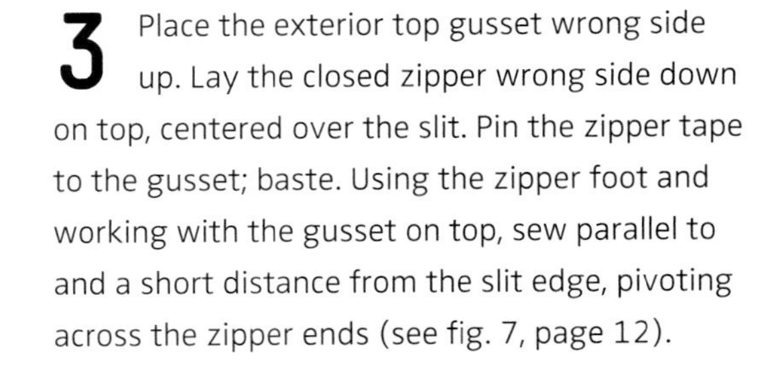

4 With the wrong sides together, pin one long edge of the exterior bottom to the straight edge of one of the main pieces; sew, using 1/4" (5 mm) seam allowance. Repeat to sew the opposite edge of the bottom to the other

main piece. With the wrong sides together, pin the ends of the top gusset to the ends of the bottom, matching the center marks (the gusset should be between the main pieces). Sew, using 1/4" (5 mm) seam allowance; leave 1/4" (5 mm) at each end of the seam unsewn. Aligning the center top marks on the gusset with the corresponding marks on the main pieces, pin and then baste the gusset to the main pieces, using 1/4" (5 mm) seam allowance. Sew together.

5 Place a zipper stop triangle at each end of the zipper (they should point down) and mark the outline of each. Apply glue inside the marked areas and to the wrong side of each stop. Also apply glue at each end of the wrong side of the zipper tab. Let dry 20 minutes. Press each triangular stop in place. Fold the zipper tab in half over the zipper pull (see photo at right).

6 On the top (longer) edge of the twill interior pocket, fold and press 3/8" (1 cm) and then 3/4" (2 cm) to the wrong side. Pin; then sew close to the first fold. On the other long edge and then on each side, fold and press 3/8" (1 cm) to the wrong side. Pin the pocket to one of the lining main pieces, placing the wrong side of the pocket against the right side of the lining and centering it about 1 1/2" (4 cm) above the bottom edge. Sew the pocket to the lining, stitching close to the side and bottom edges and reinforcing the top corners with a small triangle (see fig. 23, page 17). Divide the pocket into compartments by sewing from top to bottom parallel to the sides in one or two places.

7 With the right sides together, pin the long straight edges of the lining gussets together. Referring to the drawing below and using 1/2" (1 cm) seam allowance, sew for 2 1/2" (6 cm) at each end of the pinned edge. Press the seam allowances open, folding them back along the open area to accommodate the zipper.

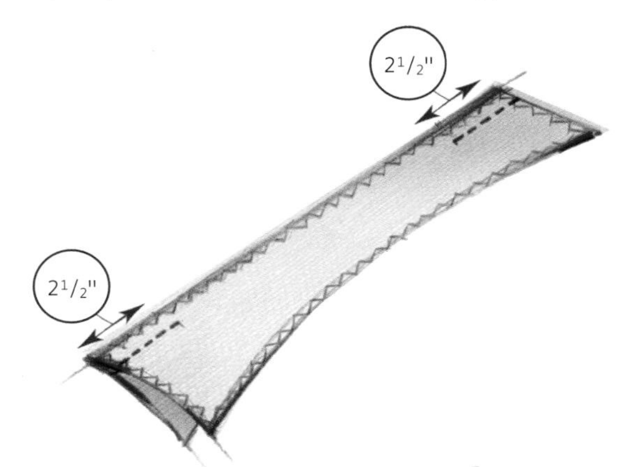

8 Working with the fabric always right sides together and using 1/2" (1 cm) seam allowance, assemble the twill lining as explained in step 4. Keep the lining wrong side out.

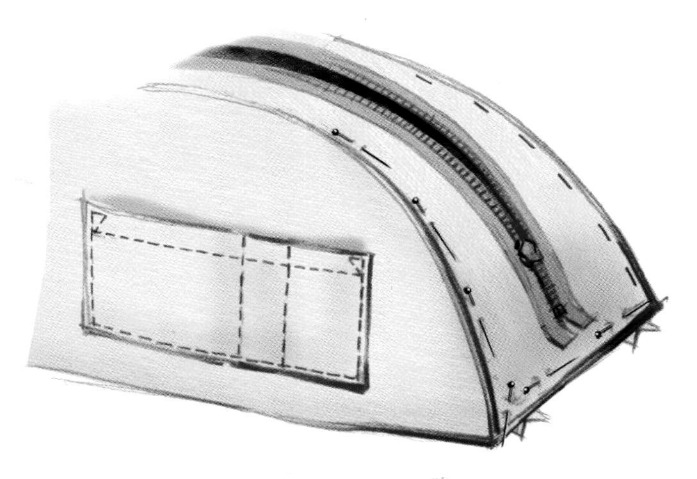

9 Insert the lining into the exterior bag; press the bottom into place and align the seams. Pin the edges of the opening in the top of the lining to the tape on each side of the zipper; then slipstitch the edges in place (see fig. 16, page 16).

Tips

Many of the seams on this project are are sewn with the fabric wrong sides together so that the edges are exposed. Make sure your cut edges are nice and neat.

To avoid leaving unsightly holes in the tablecloth pad portion of your bag, use adhesive tape or low-tack masking tape to test-fit the pieces before pinning them together.

Pin the tablecloth pad pieces together exactly on the seamlines, with the pins parallel to the edges. Pull out the pins as you sew to prevent them from being caught by the presser foot.

Textured and rubberized fabrics like the tablecloth pad may not move smoothly through your sewing machine; if they get stuck on the feed dogs they may be damaged. To prevent this, sandwich your work between pieces of tissue paper, aligning the paper edges with the edges of the fabric. Sew through all thicknesses; then, when the seam is complete, tear off the tissue paper.

Tools

Sewing essentials (see page 7),
Tailor's chalk,
Ballpoint pen,
Tracing paper and pencil (or photocopier) for flower pattern,
Household scissors,
Cutting mat,
Ruler,
Rotary cutter,
Zipper foot for your sewing machine.

Materials

- Black fabric embellished with a grid of rectangular paillettes: 17 1/2" x 27" (42 cm x 68 cm)
- Black cotton brushed twill: 29 1/4" x 38" (69 cm x 92 cm)
- Orange felt: 14" x 4" (35 cm x 10 cm)
- Lightweight batting: 26" x 8" (66 cm x 21 cm)
- Crisp interfacing (such as stencil Mylar): 2 1/2" x 21" (6 cm x 54 cm)
- 2 black zippers: one 6" (15 cm) long; one 11 1/2" (30 cm) long
- 2 metal book rings (hinged rings), 2 1/4" (6 cm) in diameter
- 1 metal ring, 5/8" (1.5 cm) in diameter
- 1 snap hook
- Thin black and orange ribbons, twisted together: 14" (35 cm) length
- Pin back (jewelry finding), for attaching the felt flower
- Black thread; Spray fabric adhesive

Faux croco

Bag dimensions: 13" (32 cm) wide x 2 1/2" (6 cm) deep x 6" (15 cm) high (excluding the handles)
Detachable pocket dimensions: 5 1/2" (14 cm) wide x 4 1/2" (11 cm) high

Prepare the pieces

Trace or photocopy the flower pattern on page 160. *Turn to page 160 to see how to arrange the pieces on your fabric.*

Paillette fabric - Mark and then cut:
2 main pieces 14" x 7" (34 cm x 17 cm);
1 bottom gusset 3 1/2" x 27" (8 cm x 68 cm);
1 detachable pocket 6 1/2" x 10" (16 cm x 24 cm).

Black twill - Mark and then cut:
4 main pieces 14" x 7" (34 cm x 17 cm);
2 bottom gussets 3 1/2" x 27" (8 cm x 68 cm);
2 top (zipper) gussets 2 1/4" x 12 1/2" (4.5 cm x 32 cm);
1 handle 6" x 26" (14 cm x 65 cm);
2 handle links 6" x 3 1/2" (14 cm x 8 cm);
1 inside pocket 8 1/2" x 6" (21 cm x 14 cm);
2 ring links: one 1 1/4" x 3 1/4" (3 cm x 8 cm) and one 1 1/4" x 1 3/4" (3 cm x 4 cm);
1 detachable pocket 6 1/2" x 10" (16 cm x 24 cm).

Batting - Mark and then cut:
2 main pieces 13" x 5 1/2" (32 cm x 14 cm);
1 gusset 2 1/2" x 25" (6 cm x 25 cm).

Interfacing - Mark and then cut 1 piece the size indicated in the materials list.

Felt - Mark and then cut 3 flowers.

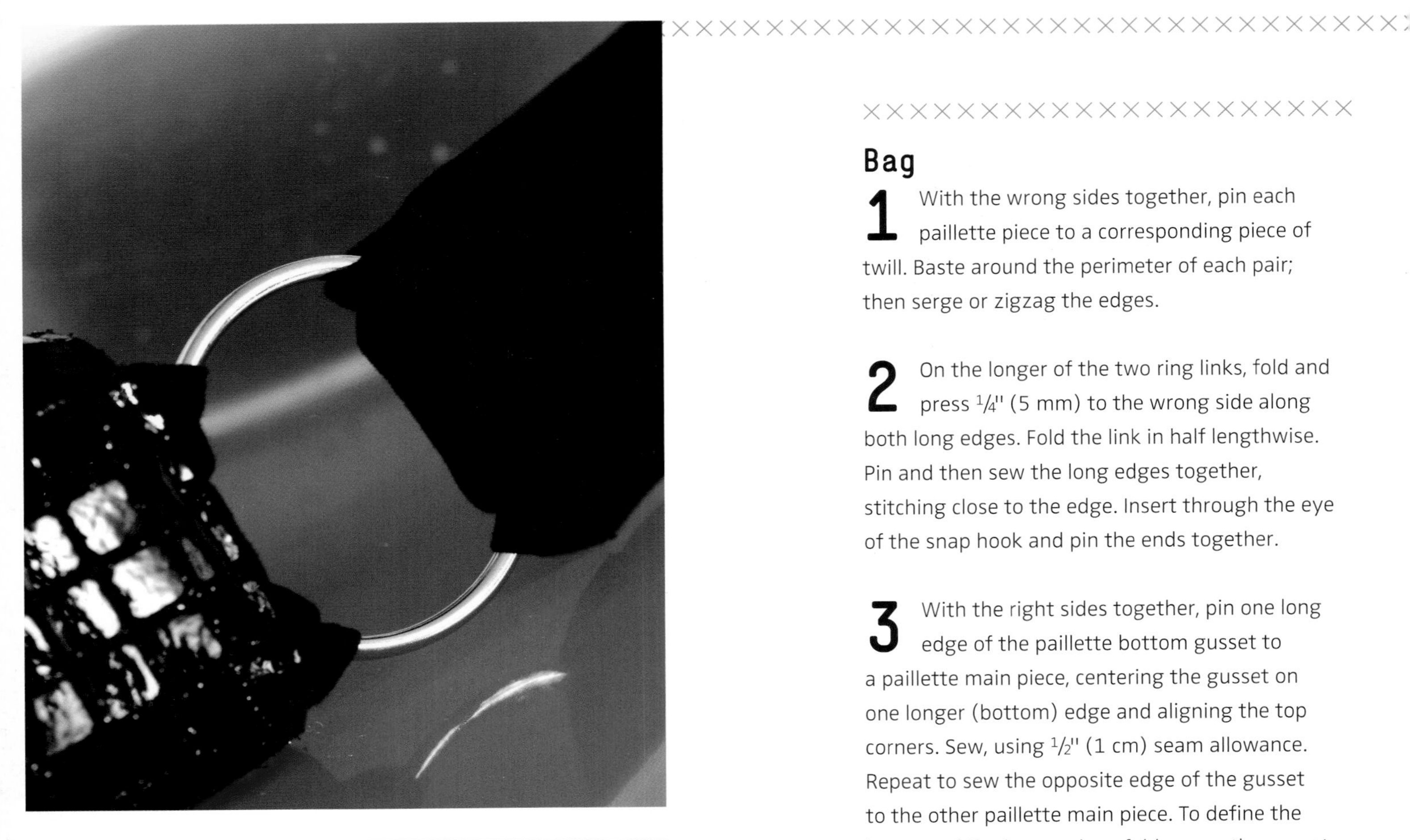

Bag

1 With the wrong sides together, pin each paillette piece to a corresponding piece of twill. Baste around the perimeter of each pair; then serge or zigzag the edges.

2 On the longer of the two ring links, fold and press 1/4" (5 mm) to the wrong side along both long edges. Fold the link in half lengthwise. Pin and then sew the long edges together, stitching close to the edge. Insert through the eye of the snap hook and pin the ends together.

3 With the right sides together, pin one long edge of the paillette bottom gusset to a paillette main piece, centering the gusset on one longer (bottom) edge and aligning the top corners. Sew, using 1/2" (1 cm) seam allowance. Repeat to sew the opposite edge of the gusset to the other paillette main piece. To define the bottom of the bag, make a fold across the gusset at each of the bottom corners and topstitch close to the fold.

4 For the lining, pin the remaining twill bottom gusset and main pieces together in the same way. Before you sew, put the assembled link and snap hook into the pinned bag and slide the end of the link through one of the side seams, about 2½" (6 cm) below the top edge (the hook should be against the right side of the lining). Sew the lining seams and then fold and topstitch the bottom corners as in step 3.

5 On the top (longer) edge of the interior pocket, fold and press ⅜" (1 cm) and then 1" (2.5 cm) to the wrong side. Pin, then sew close to the first fold. On the other long edge and then on each side, fold and press ⅜" (1 cm) to the wrong side.

6 Pin the pocket to the lining main piece that has the snap hook, placing the wrong side of the pocket against the right side of the lining and placing it about ½" (1 cm) above the bottom and ½" (1 cm) from the seam opposite the hook. Sew the pocket to the lining, stitching close to the side and bottom edges and reinforcing the top corners with a small triangle (see fig. 23, page 17). Divide the pocket into compartments by sewing from top to bottom parallel to the sides in several places.

7 On one long edge of each top gusset, fold and then press ½" (1 cm) to the wrong side. Place the longer zipper right side up on your work surface. With the right side up, align the folded edge of one gusset along the center of the zipper teeth. Place the second gusset opposite the first. Baste the gussets to the zipper tape, and then, using the zipper foot, sew ⅜" (5 mm) from the folds (see fig. 7, page 12). At each end, fold the gusset and zipper tape to the wrong side, aligning the edge of the gusset with the zipper stops; stitch close to the folded edge.

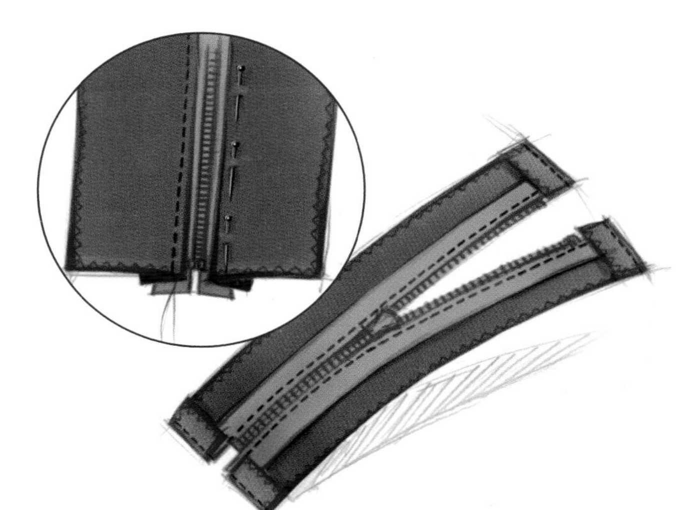

8 Referring to the drawing below and placing the right sides of the fabric together, assemble the top gusset and lining: Overlap and center one long edge of the gusset 1" (2.5 cm) below the top of the lining; sew close to the edge of the gusset. Open the zipper. Sew the opposite long edge of the gusset to the opposite edge of the lining in the same way. Working through the open zipper, fold each gusset down so its wrong side is against the right side of the lining, covering the seam just made; topstitch close to the fold.

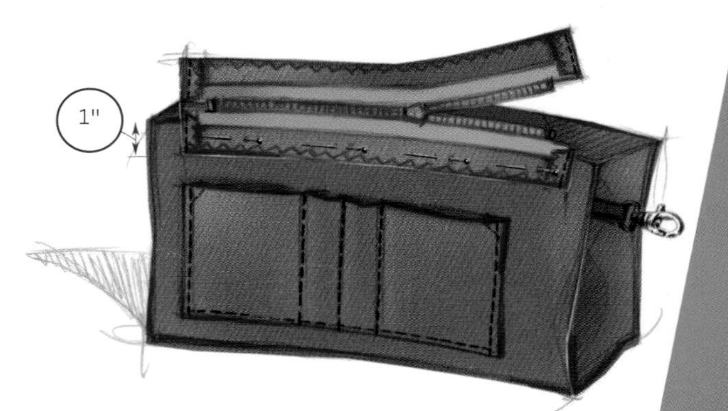

9 With the right sides together, fold each of the handle links in half, bringing the short edges together. Pin and then, using ½" (1 cm) seam allowance, sew the short edges together to form a tube. Press the seam allowances open and turn each link right side out. Center the seam on the opposite face of the tube and press again. Topstitch close to each fold. Then fold each link in half, aligning the open edges; baste.

10 Along the top edge of the paillette bag and of the lining, fold ½" (1 cm) to the wrong side; crease with your fingers. Turn the paillette bag right side out. Mist the wrong side of each batting piece with spray adhesive; then insert into the bag, aligning against the corresponding section and placing the top edge of the batting below the folded allowance at the top of the bag. Press the layers between your hands to adhere. Make sure the lining is wrong side out. Insert it into the paillette bag; align the top edges. Referring to the drawing below, insert one of the handle links between the lining and batting at the top of each gusset; let the link stand ⅝" (1.5 cm) above the edge. Pin and then baste the bags together along the top. Working through the open zipper, sew the paillette and lining bags together close to the top edge.

⅝"

11 Fold the handle in half lengthwise, wrong side out. Pin and then, using ½" (1 cm) seam allowance, sew the long edges together to form a tube. Press the seam allowances open and turn the tube right side out. Center the seam on the opposite face of the tube and press again. Slide the piece of interfacing inside the handle, centering it between the open ends. At each end, fold the fabric toward the side with the seam, folding first ½" (1 cm) and then folding again so the first fold is adjacent to the end of the interfacing. Sew close to the edge of the first fold.

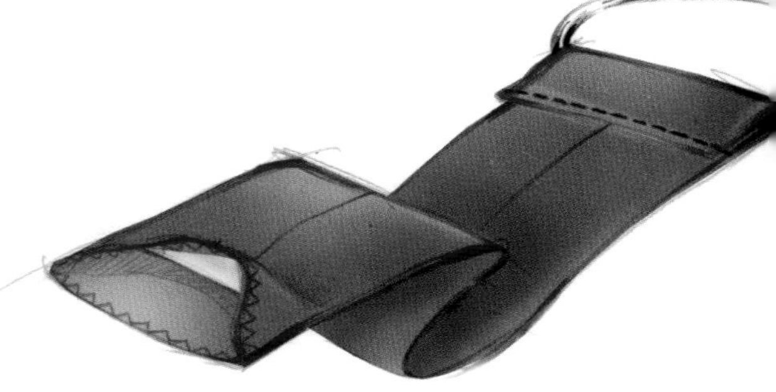

12 Open the book rings. Slide each through one end of the handle and then through one of the handle links on the bag; close each ring.

13 Fold two of the felt flowers in quarters. By hand, sew them together at their point. Then sew them to the center of the third flower. Sew the assembled flower to the pin back, catching the twisted ribbon between the flower and back. Pin the ribbon at the base of the handle on one side of the bag.

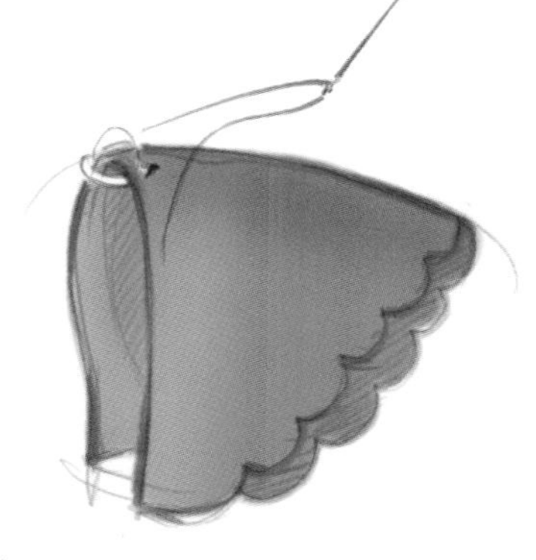

Pout

Detachable pocket

1 Following step 2 for the bag, construct the smaller ring link. Insert it through the small ring and fold in half, bringing the ends together.

2 Back the paillette pocket with a piece of twill as in step 1 for the bag. On each short edge, fold ½" (1 cm) to the twill side, and crease the fold with your finger. Referring to the drawing below, pin the remaining zipper between the folded edges of the pocket, leaving the zipper teeth exposed and making sure the pocket extends equally at each end of the zipper; baste. Using the zipper foot, sew the pocket to the zipper tape.

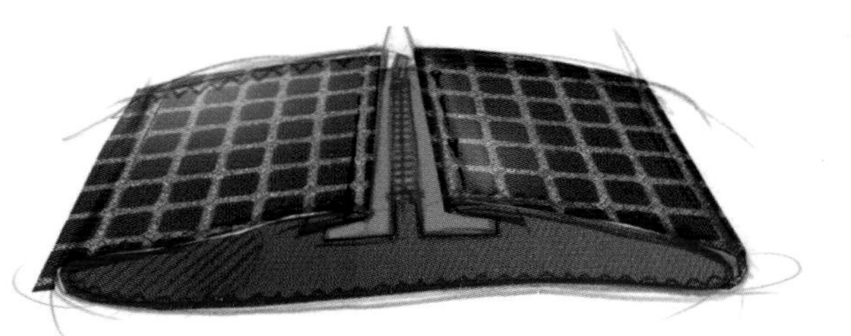

3 Open the zipper and then turn the pocket wrong side out. Fold the pocket so the zipper is centered on the opposite face as shown below. Slide the assembled ring link between the layers, aligning the link ends with the end of the pocket about ⅝" (1.5 cm) from one of the folded edges. Pin and then sew each open end of the pocket closed, using ½" (1 cm) seam allowance. Turn the pocket right side out and close the zipper. Clip the pocket to the snap hook inside the bag.

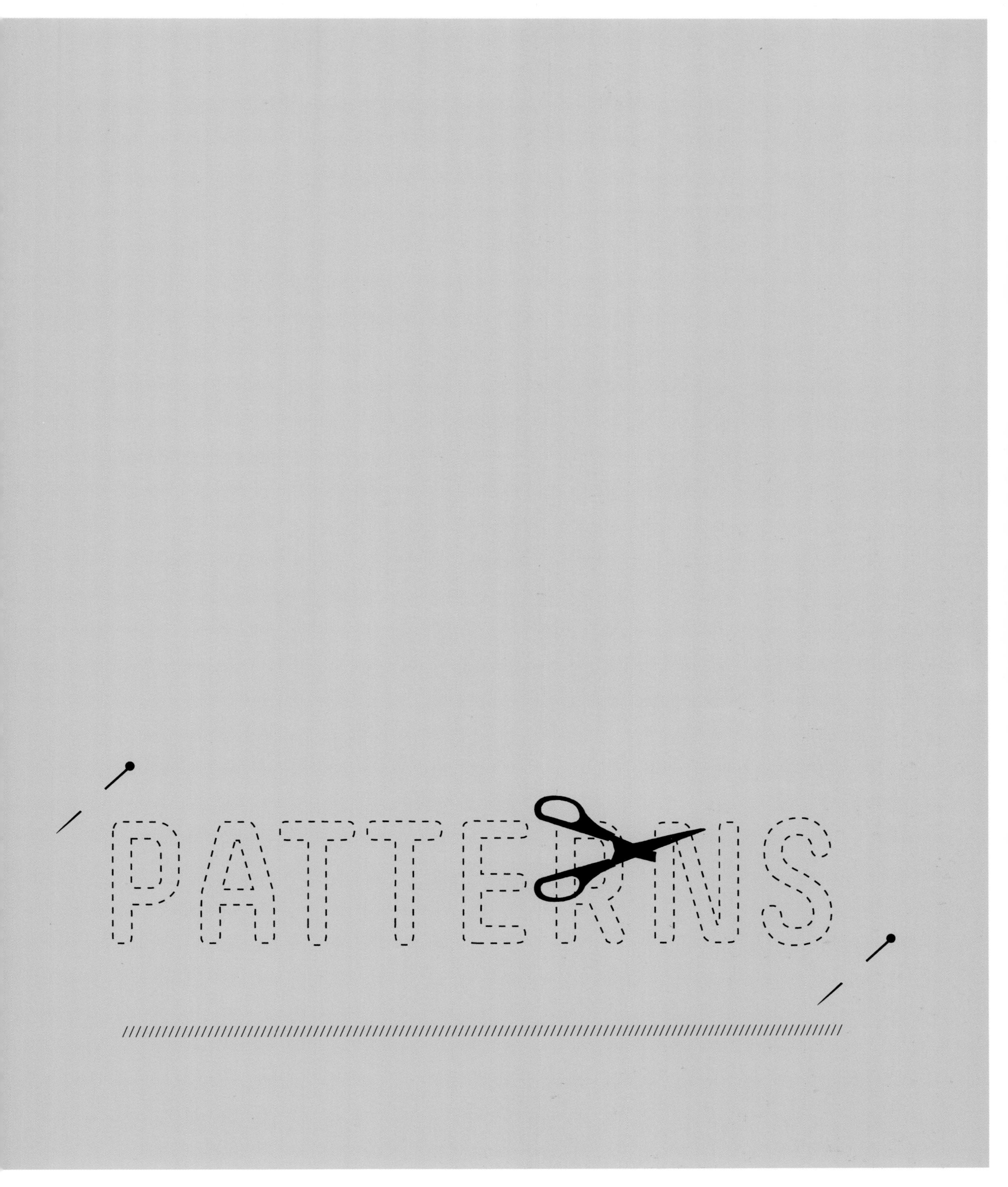
PATTERNS

Felt Kelly

page 18

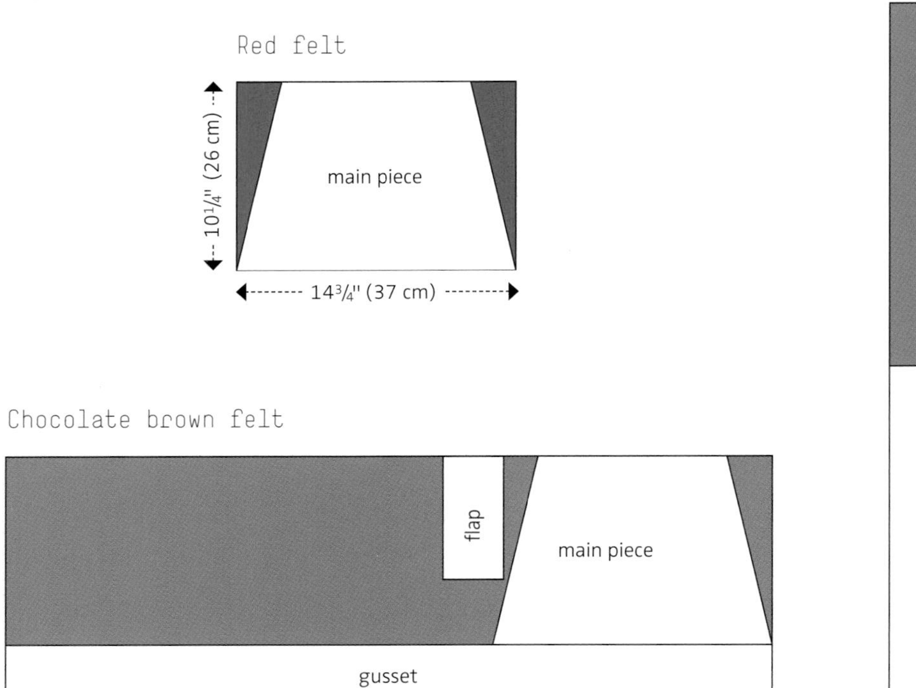

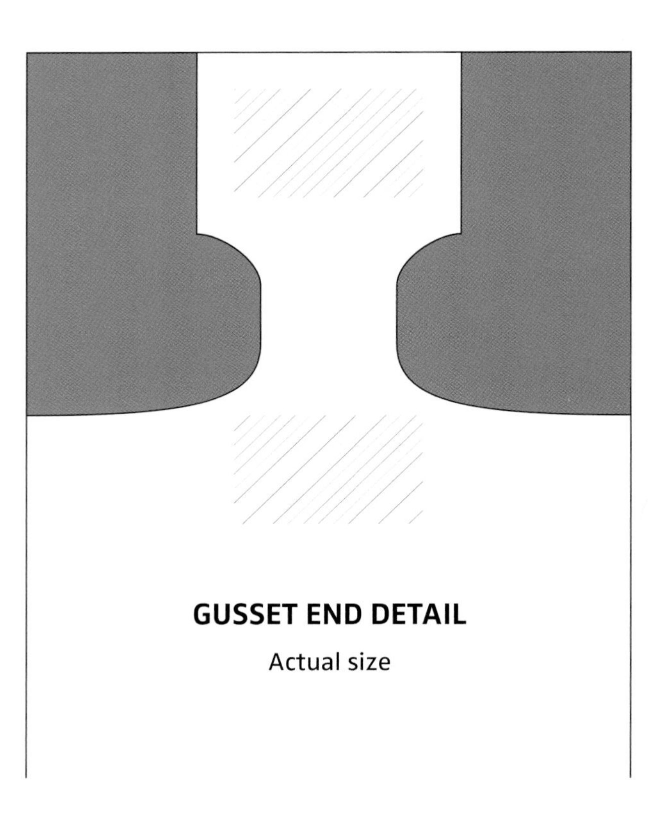

areas to be glued

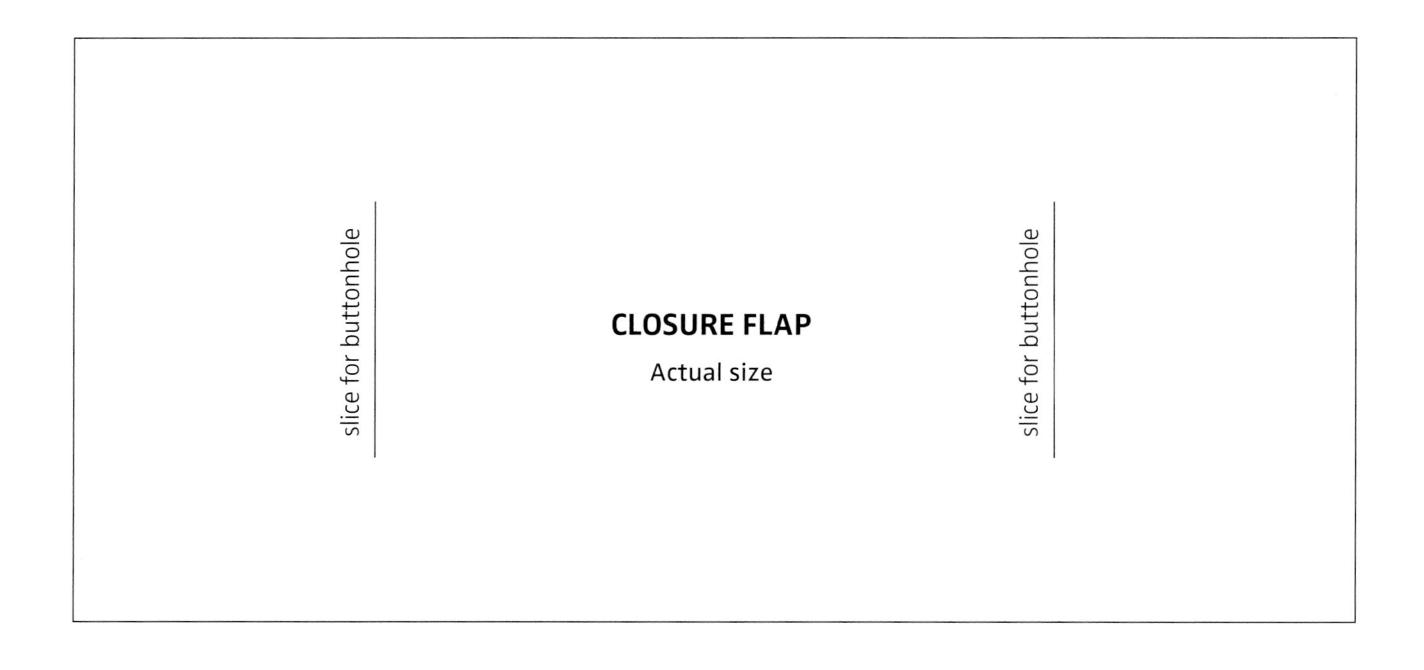

Felt Kelly

page 18

Little flowers

page 22

Suspender satchel

page 26

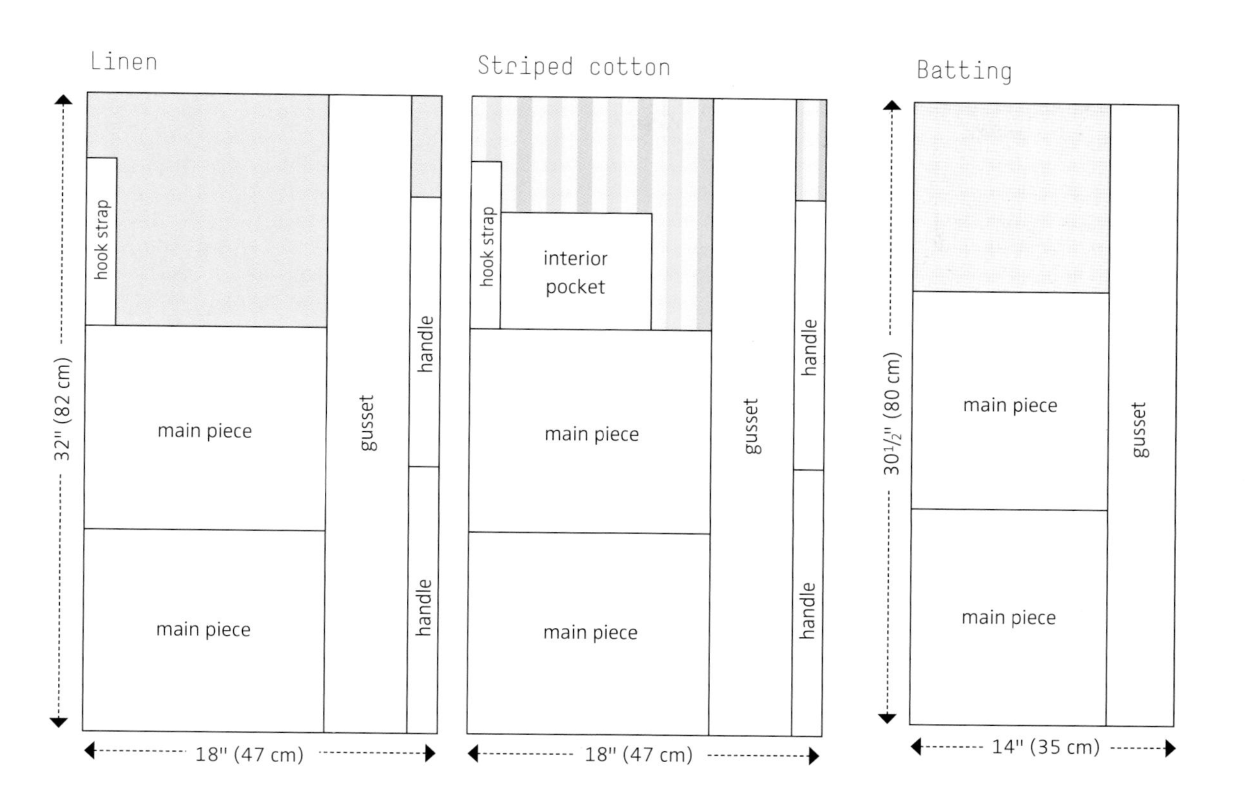

Country print tote

page 42

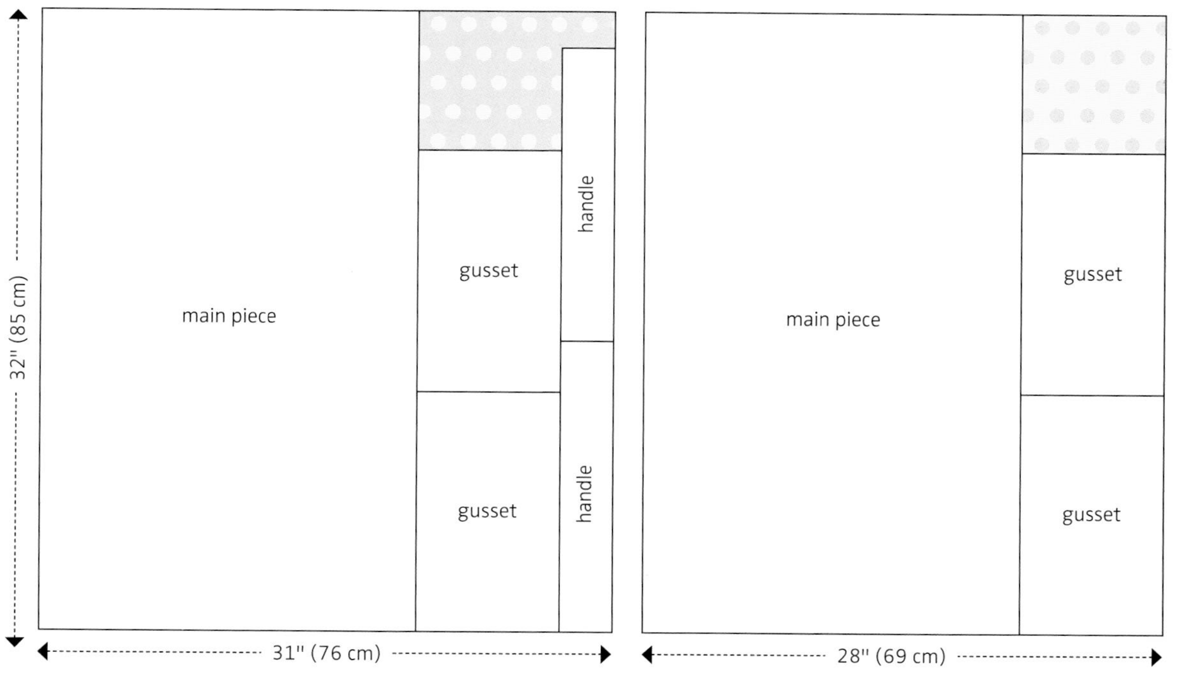

Smart carryall

page 50

Love me, love me not

page 46

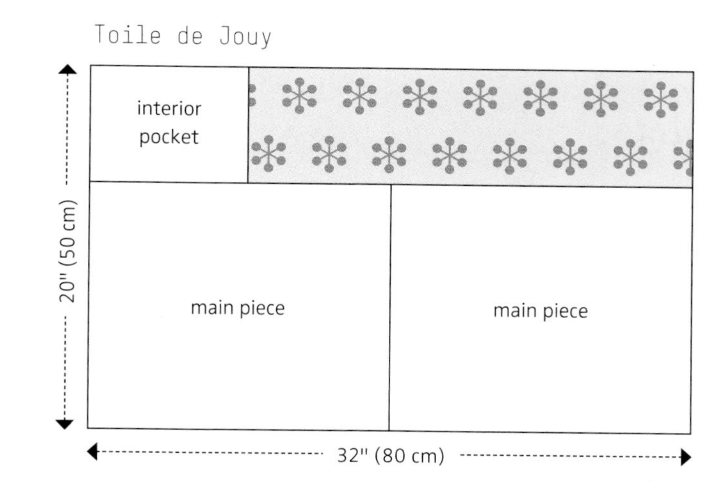

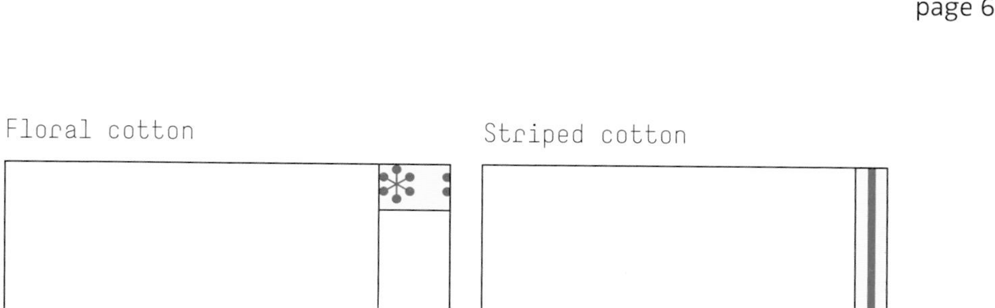

Tsarina bag

page 56

Picadilly Circus

page 60

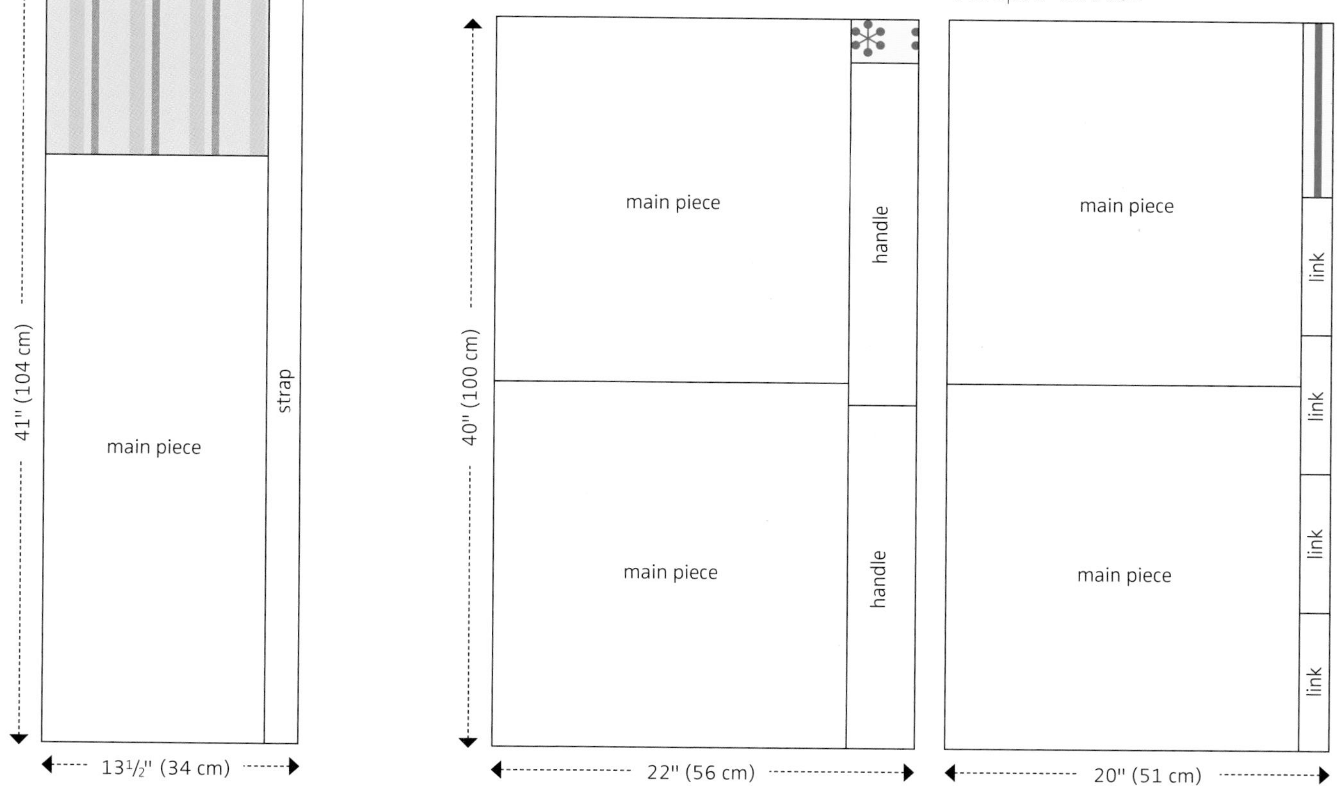

Dots and feathers

page 66

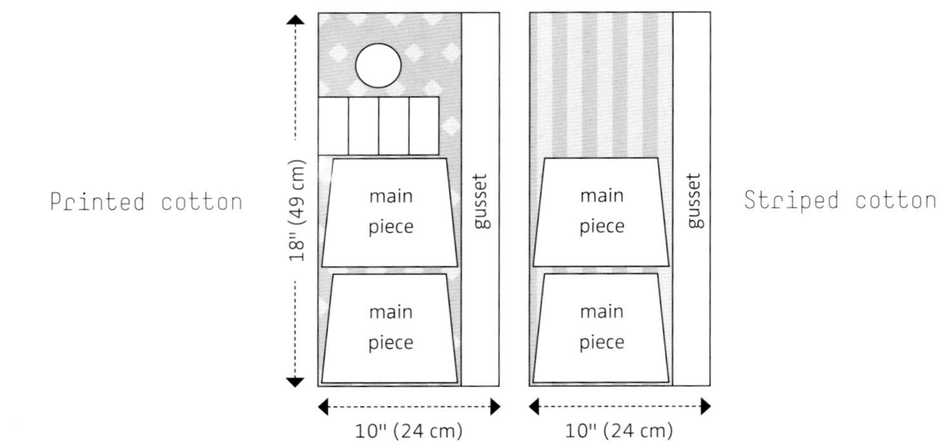

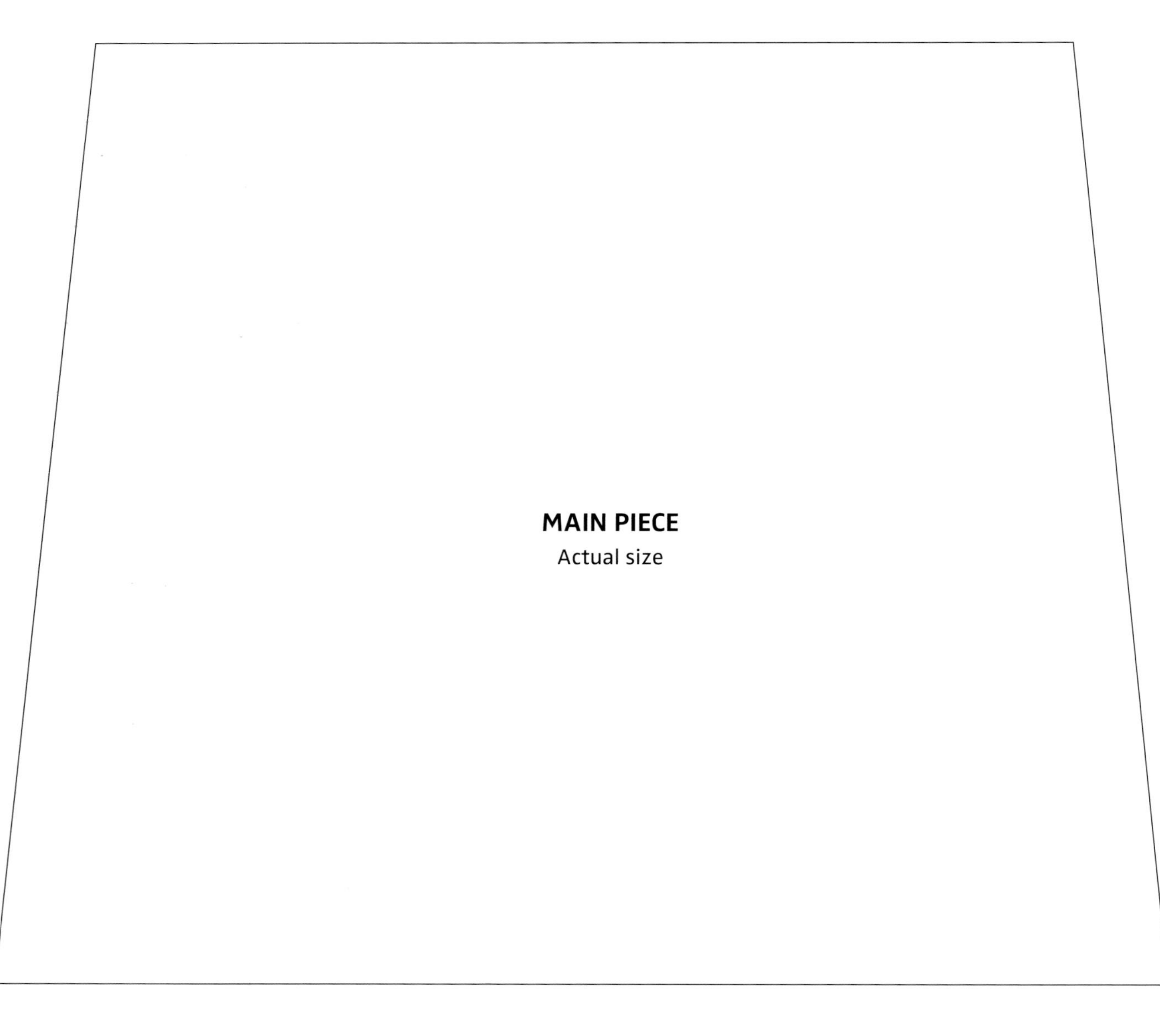

page 70

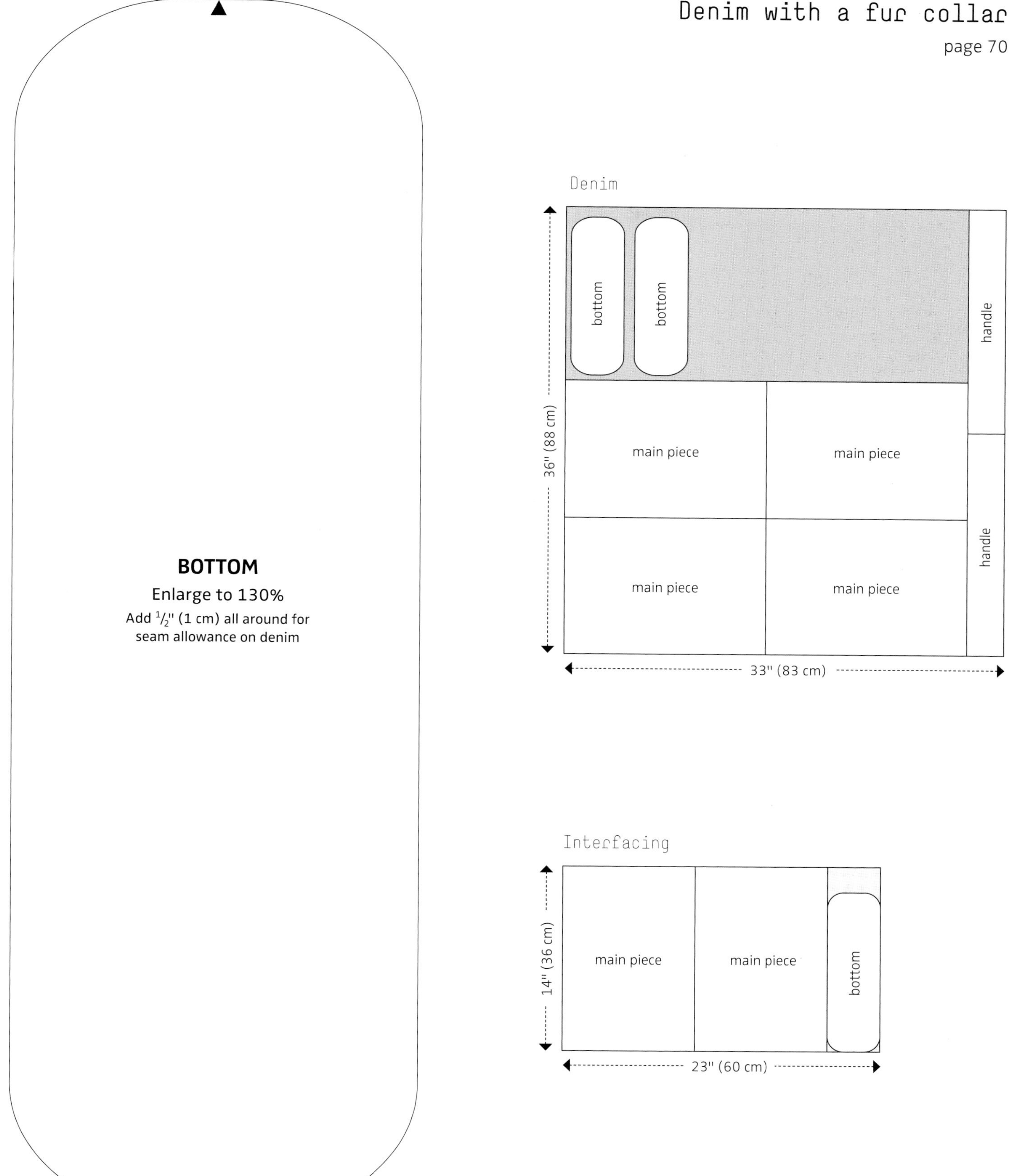
BOTTOM
Enlarge to 130%
Add 1/2" (1 cm) all around for seam allowance on denim
Denim
bottom
bottom
handle
main piece
main piece
handle
main piece
main piece
36" (88 cm)
33" (83 cm)
Interfacing
main piece
main piece
bottom
14" (36 cm)
23" (60 cm)

Carry-along shopping tote

page 74

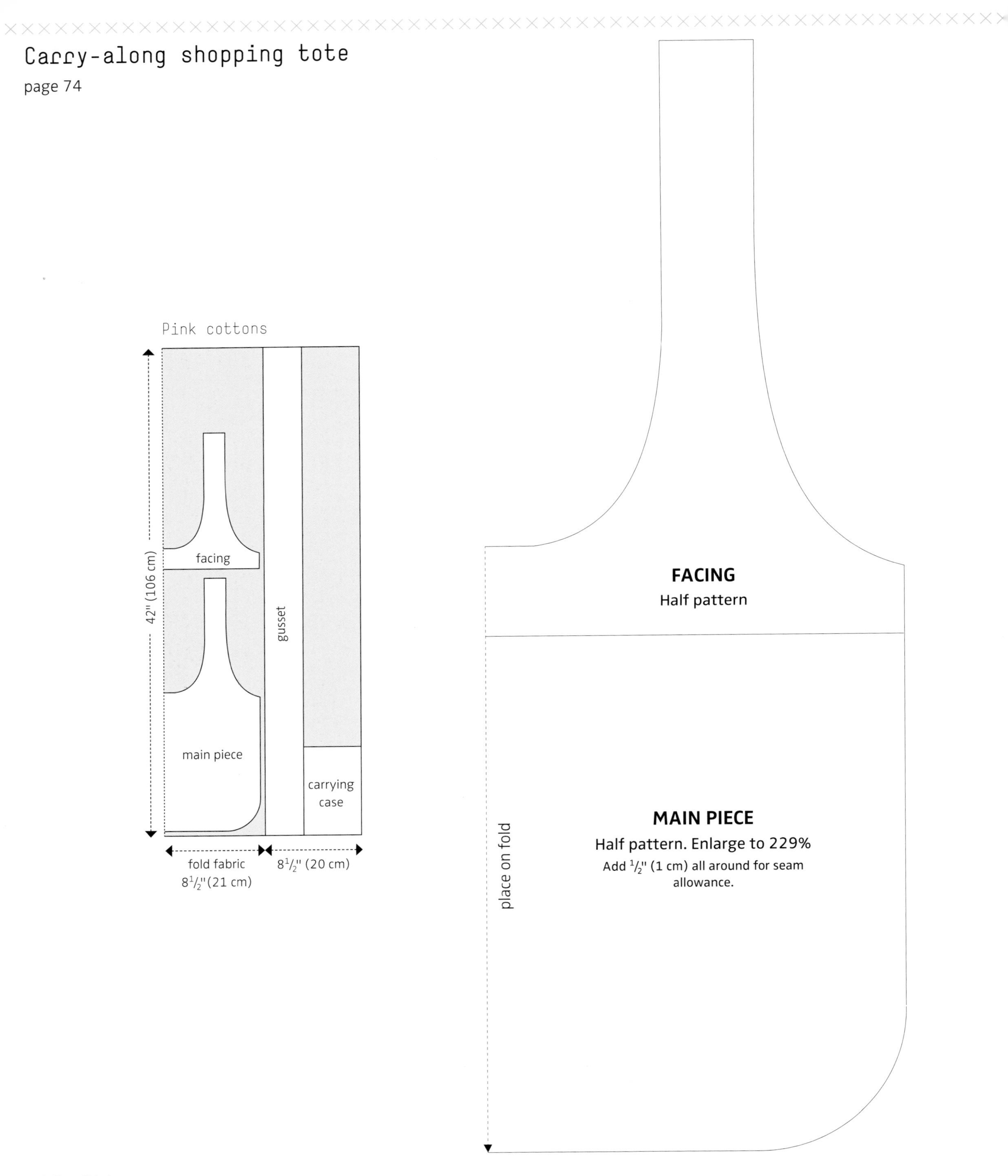

Summer stripe

page 80

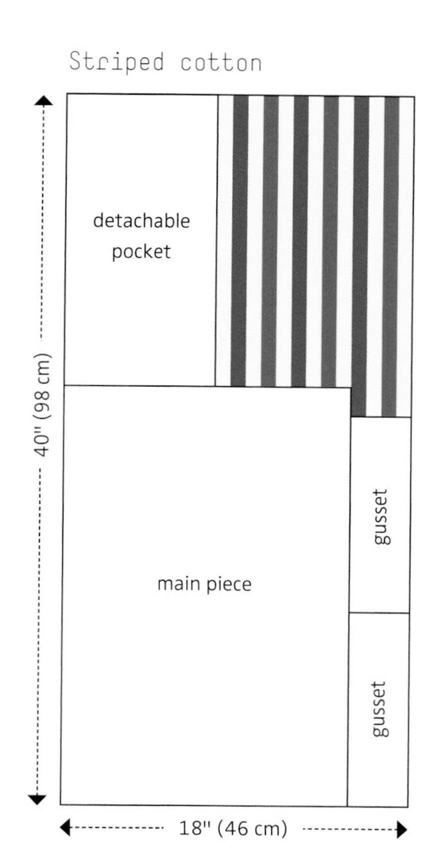

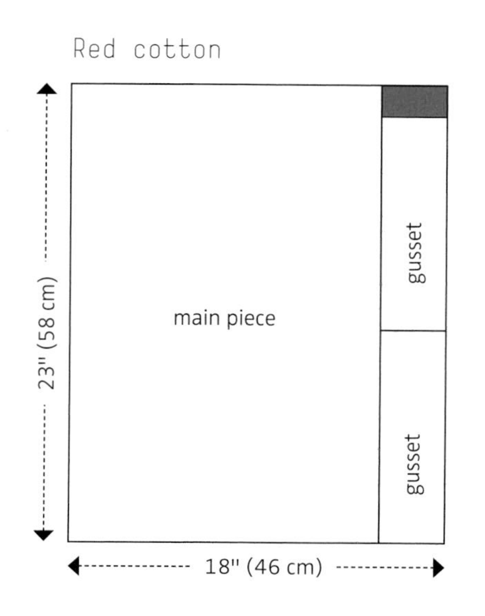

Theater or opera?

page 86

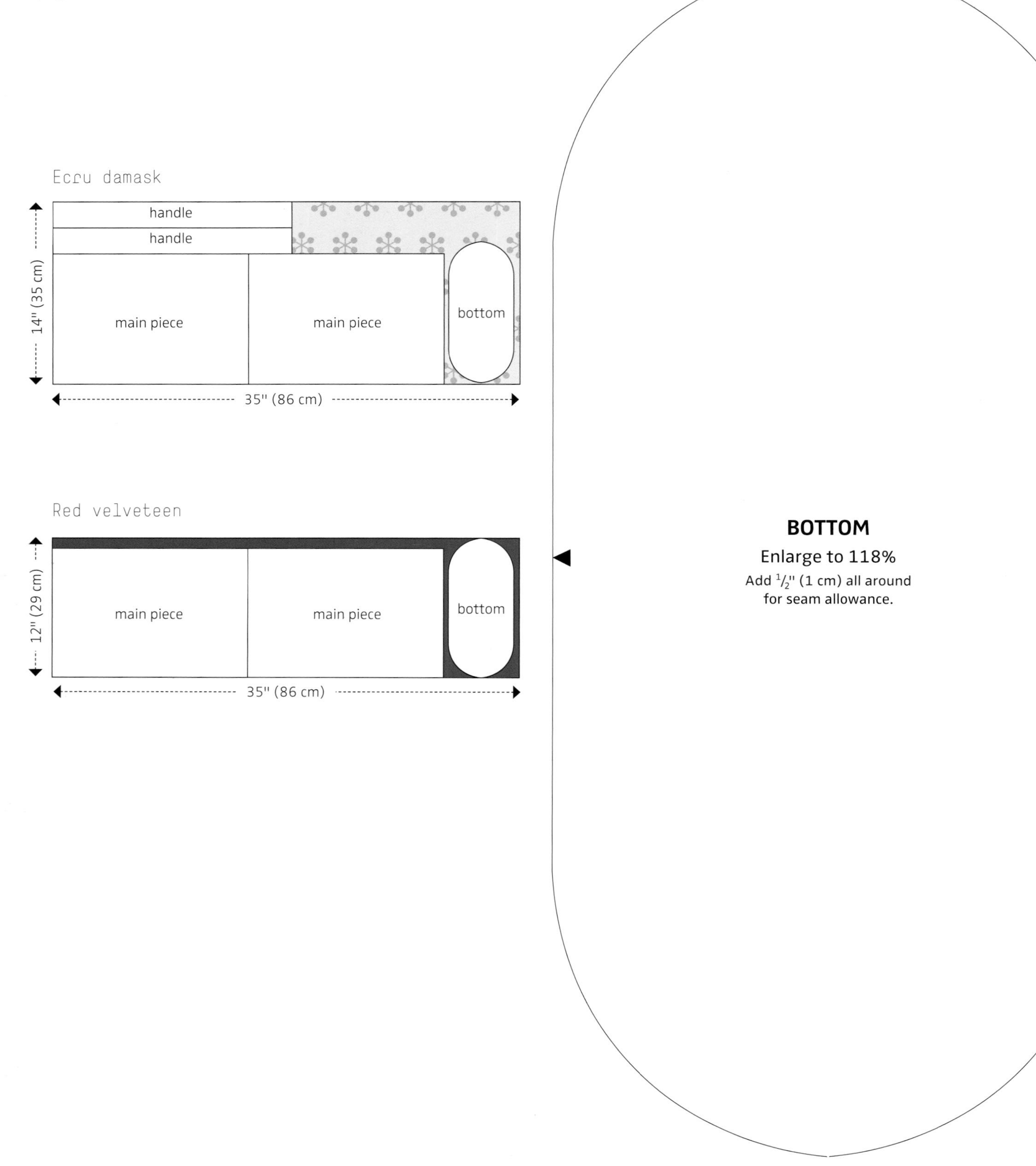

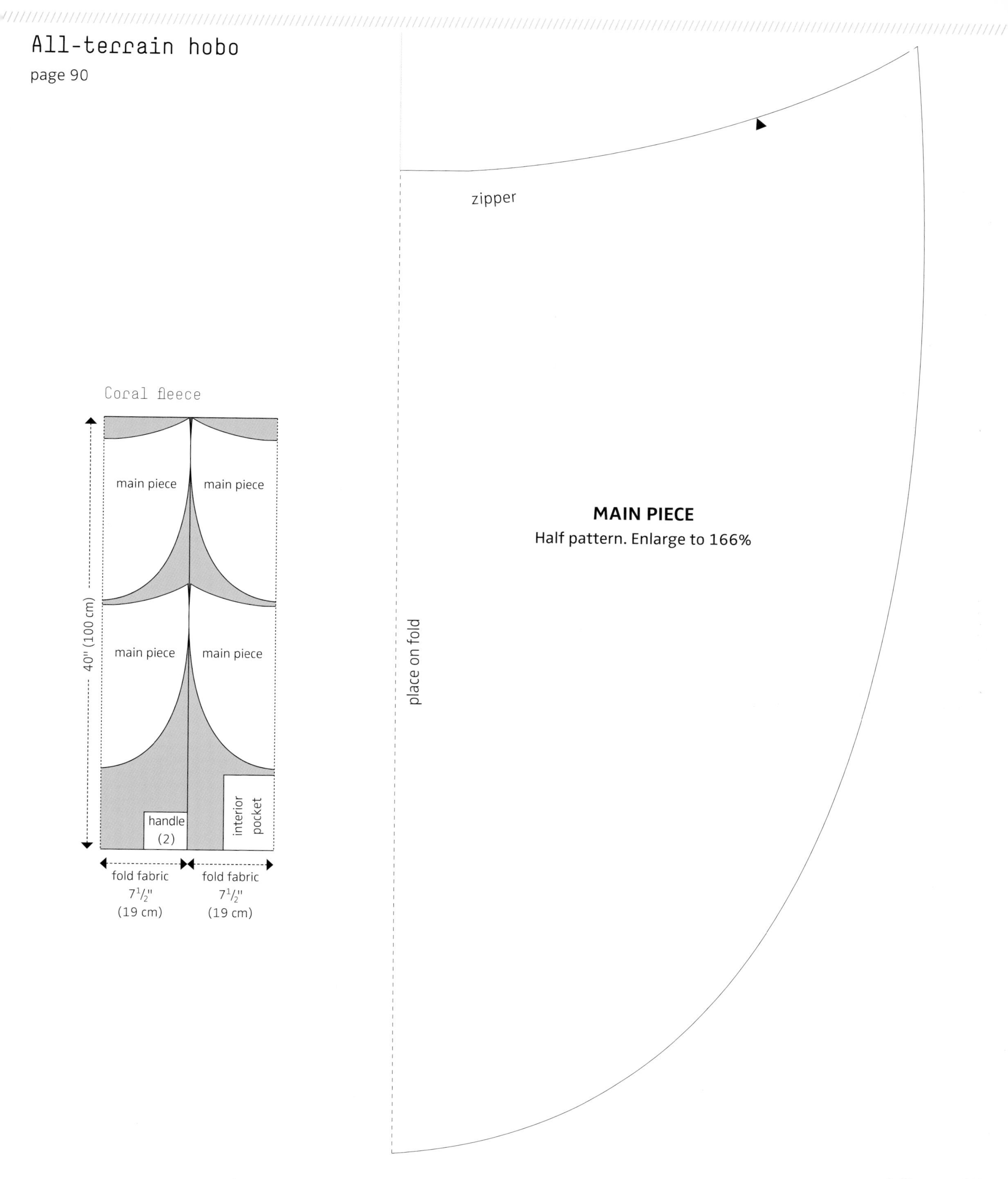
All-terrain hobo
page 90
Coral fleece
40" (100 cm)
main piece
main piece
main piece
main piece
handle
(2)
interior
pocket
fold fabric
$7^1/_2$"
(19 cm)
fold fabric
$7^1/_2$"
(19 cm)
zipper
place on fold
MAIN PIECE
Half pattern. Enlarge to 166%

Clever bucket bag

page 96

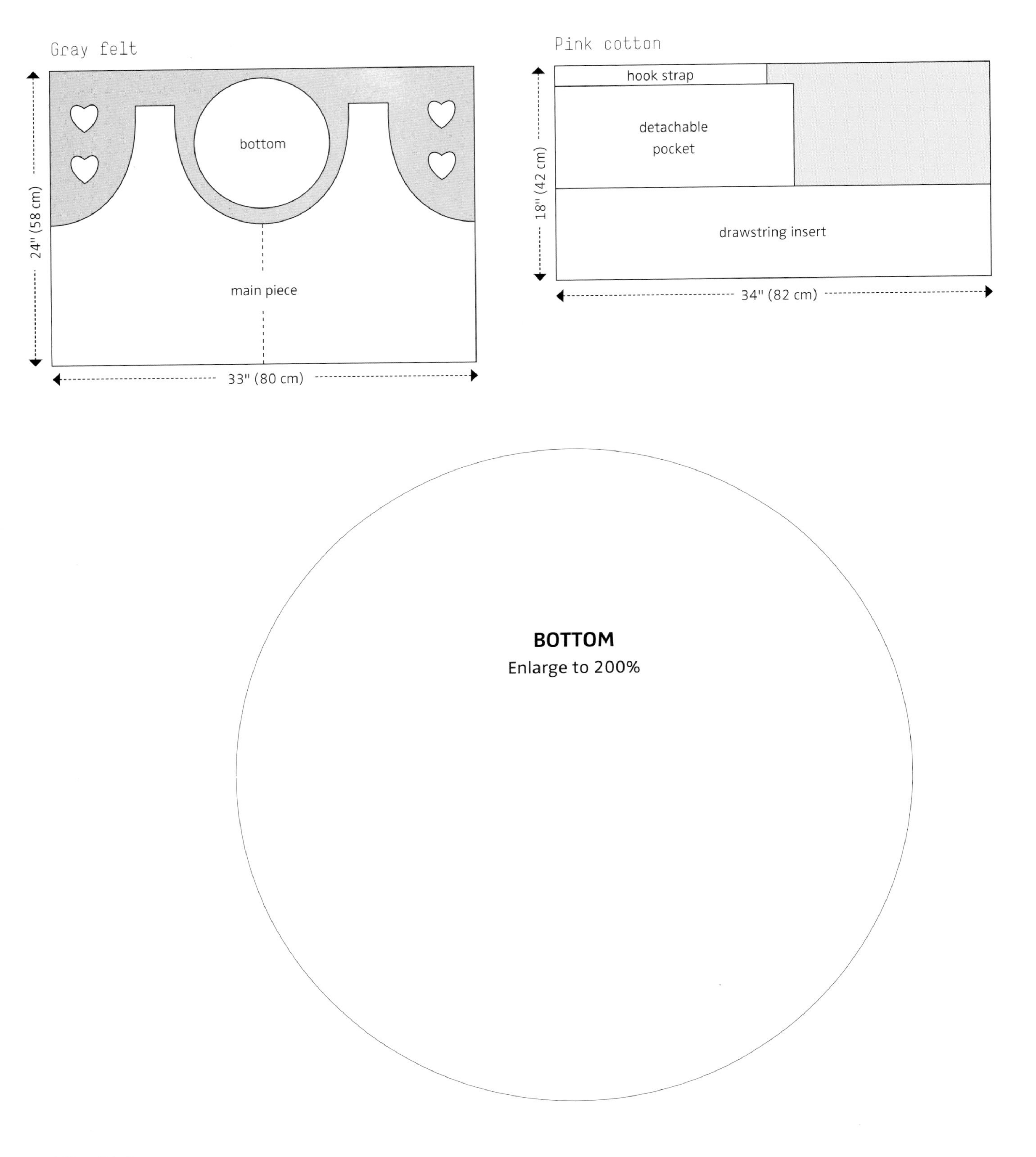

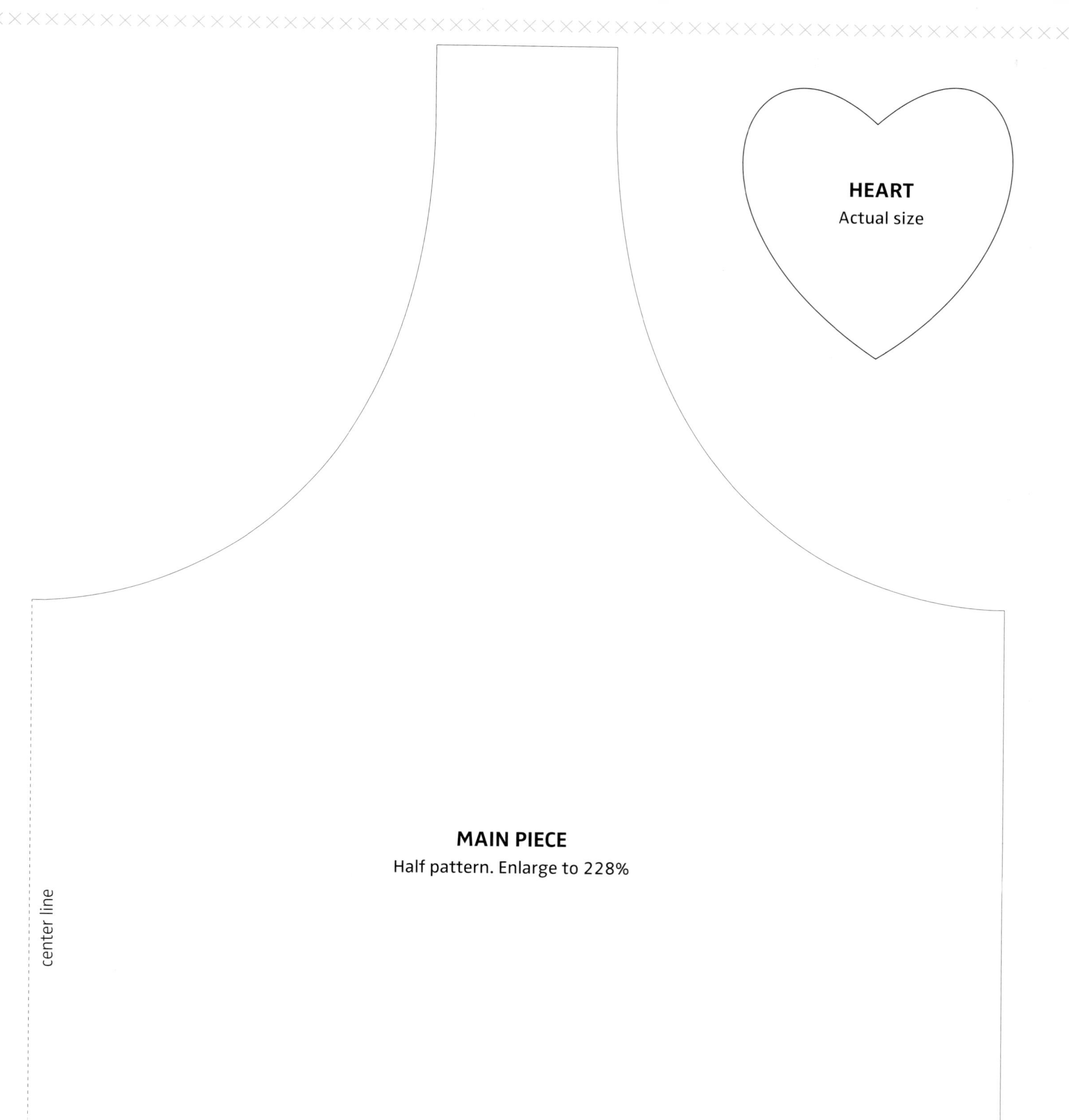
HEART
Actual size
MAIN PIECE
Half pattern. Enlarge to 228%
center line

Little black tote-plus

page 102

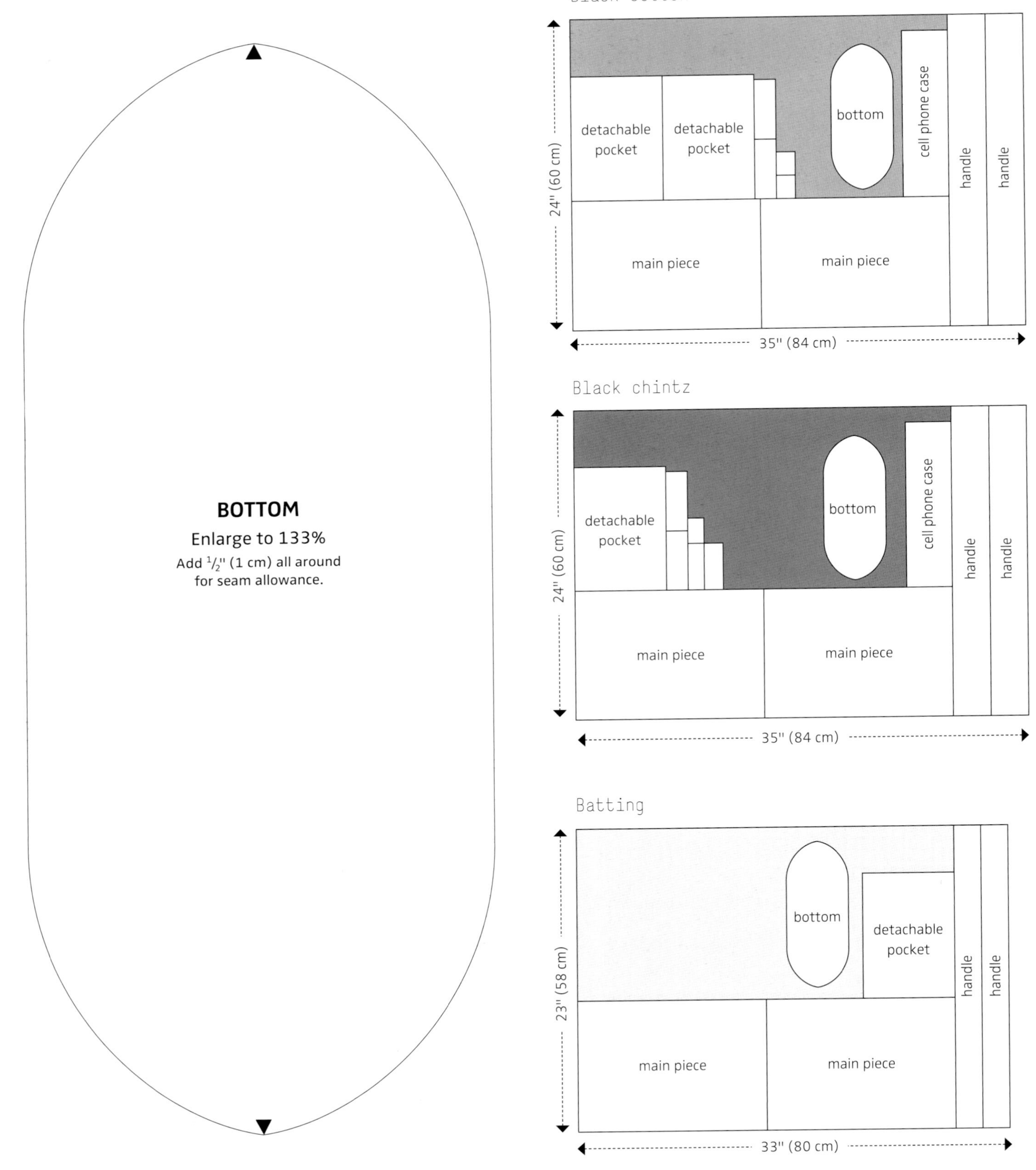

City bag

page 110

Purple felt

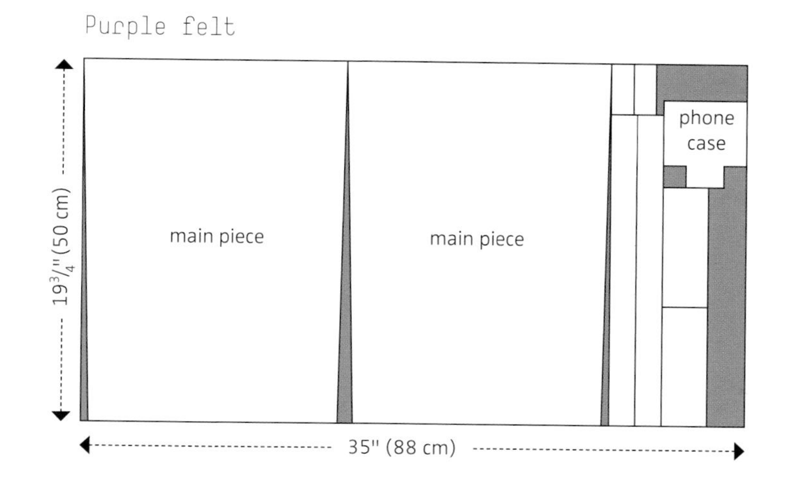

Yellow rubber

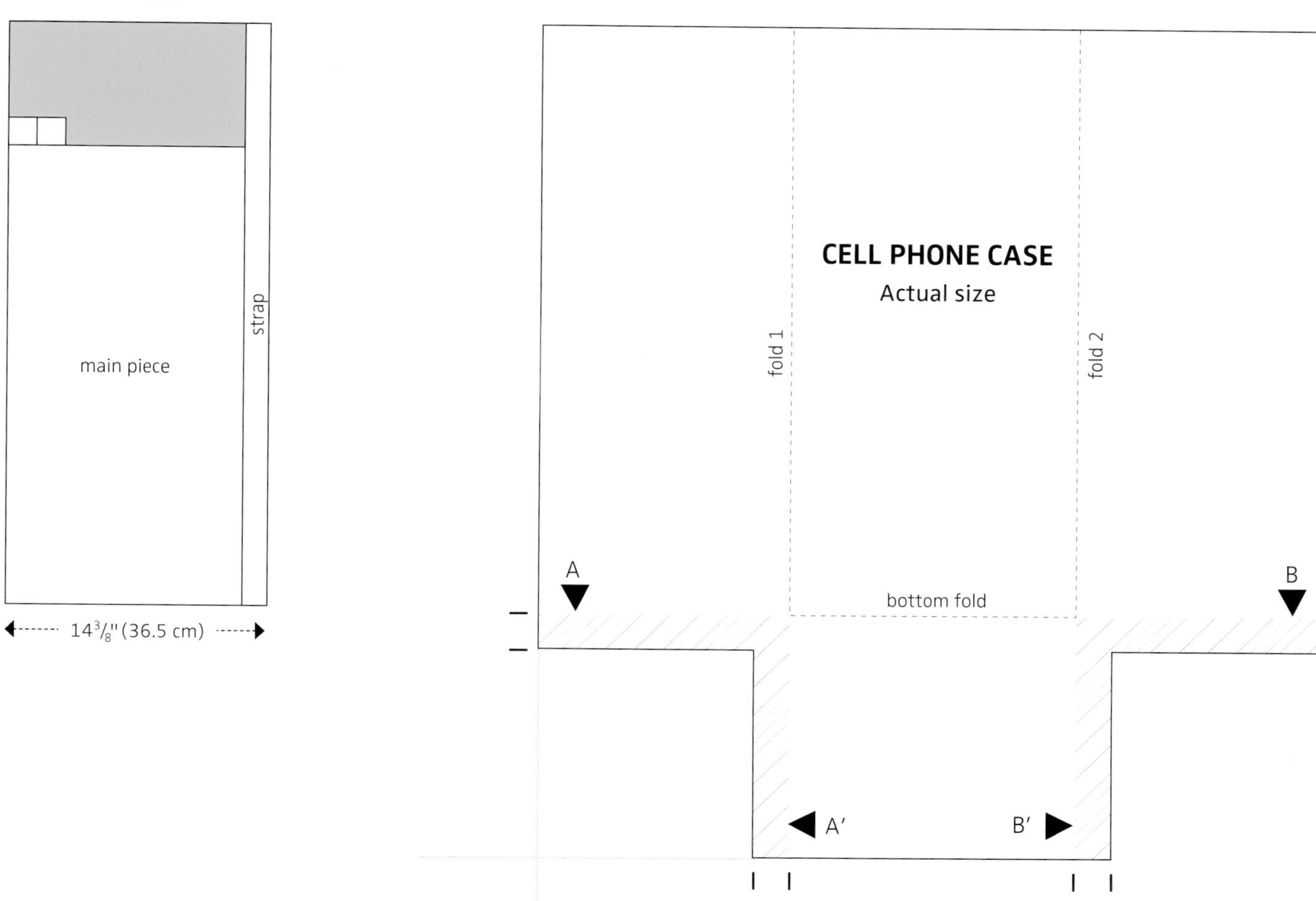

City bag

page 110

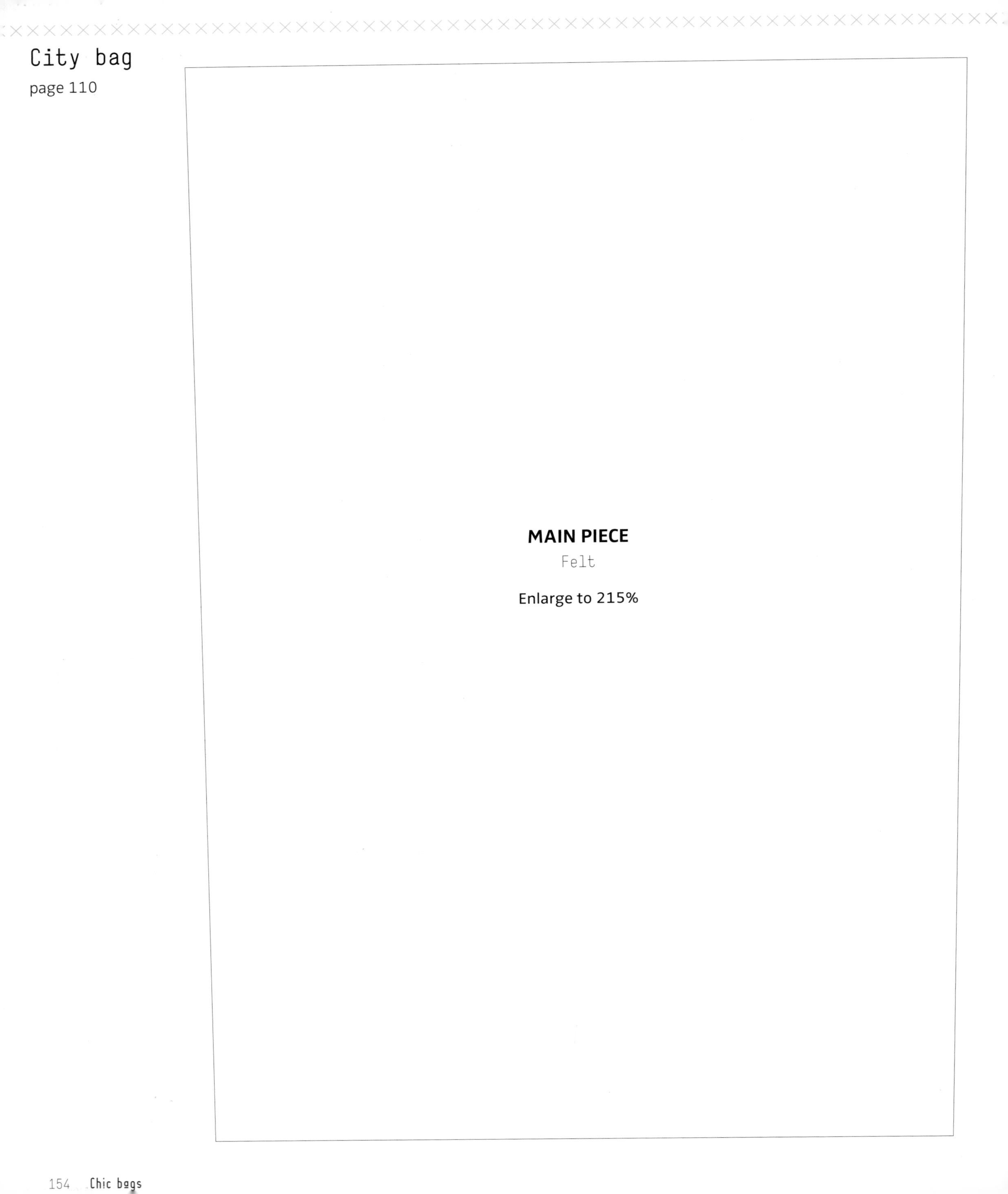

Aqua backpack

page 116

Aqua glazed fabric

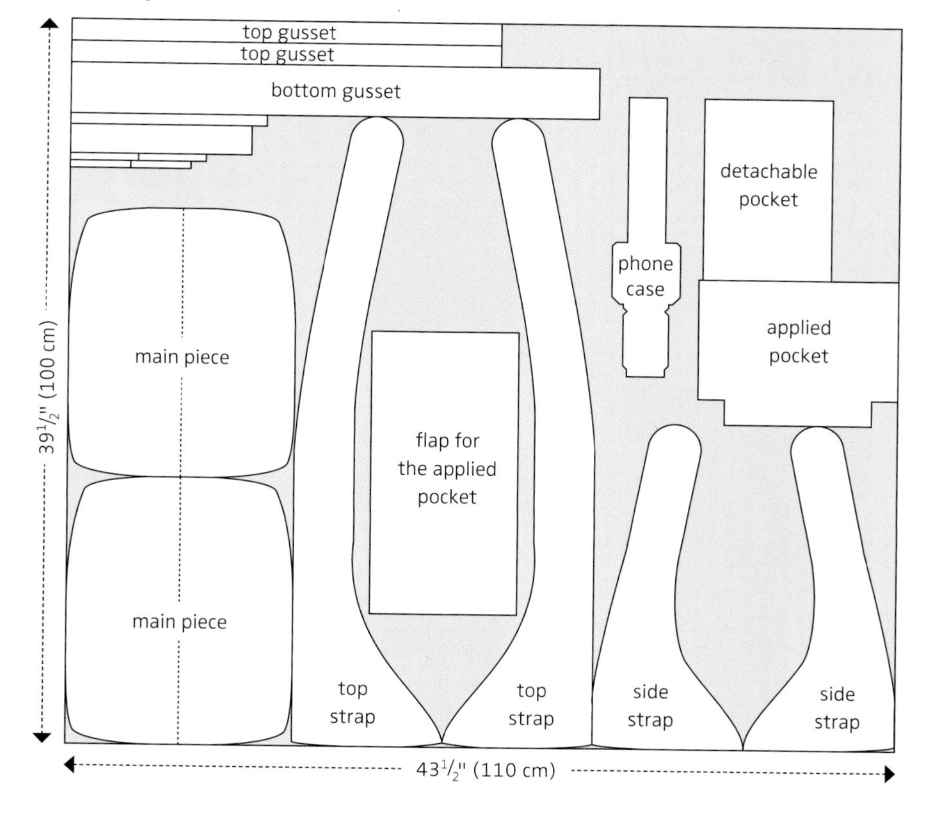

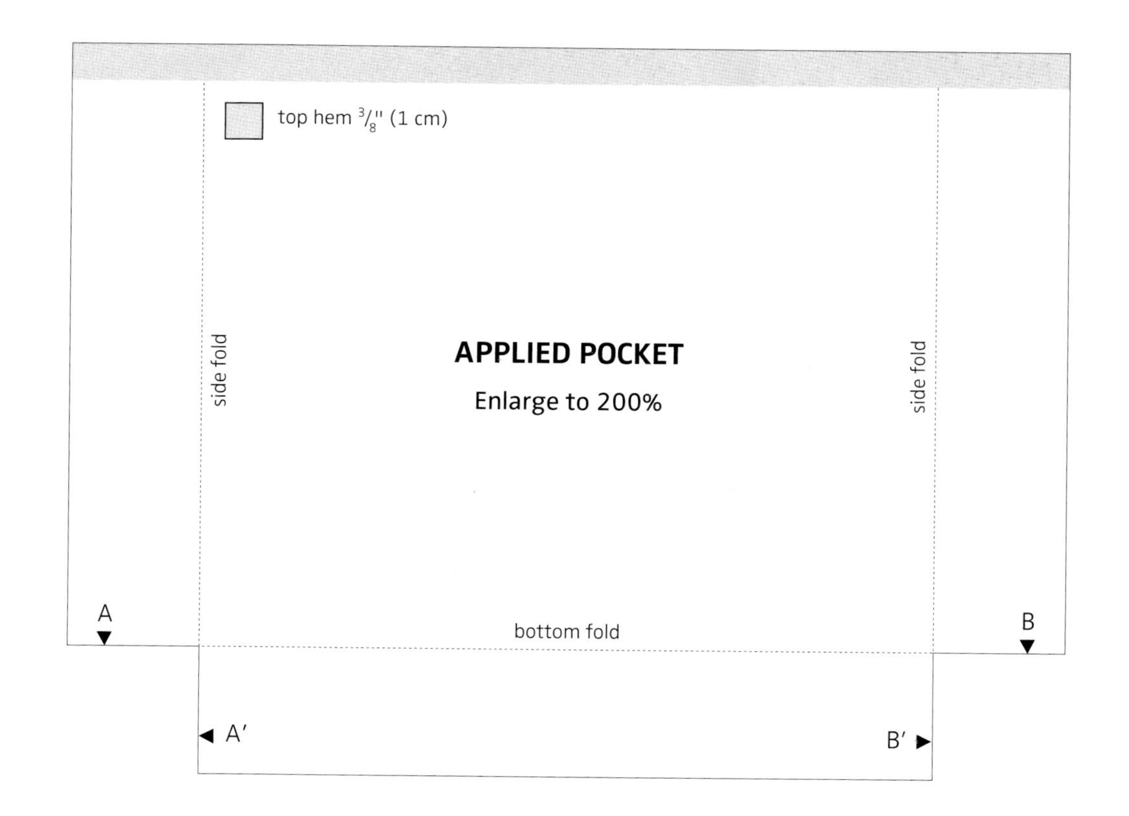

Aqua backpack

page 116

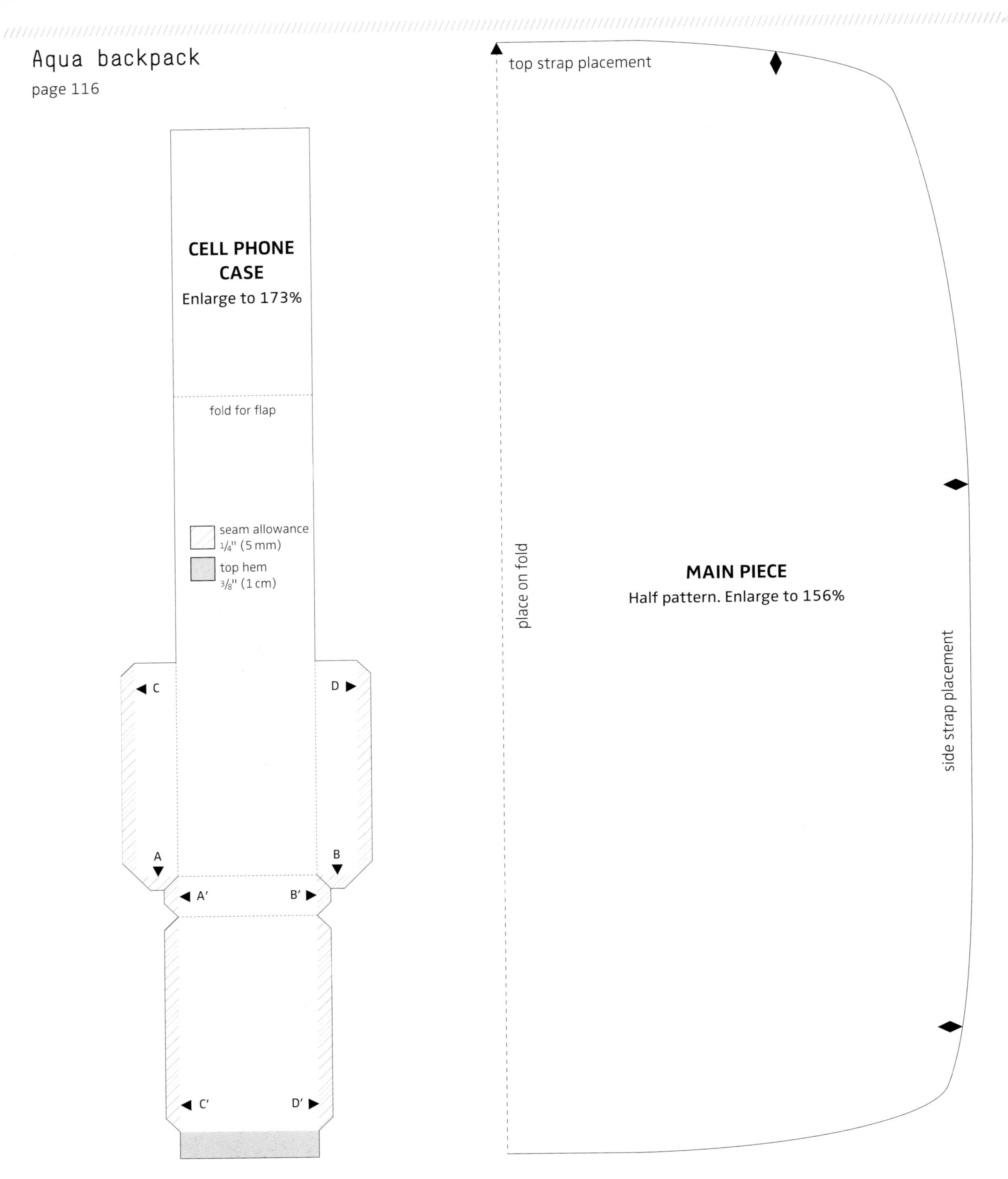

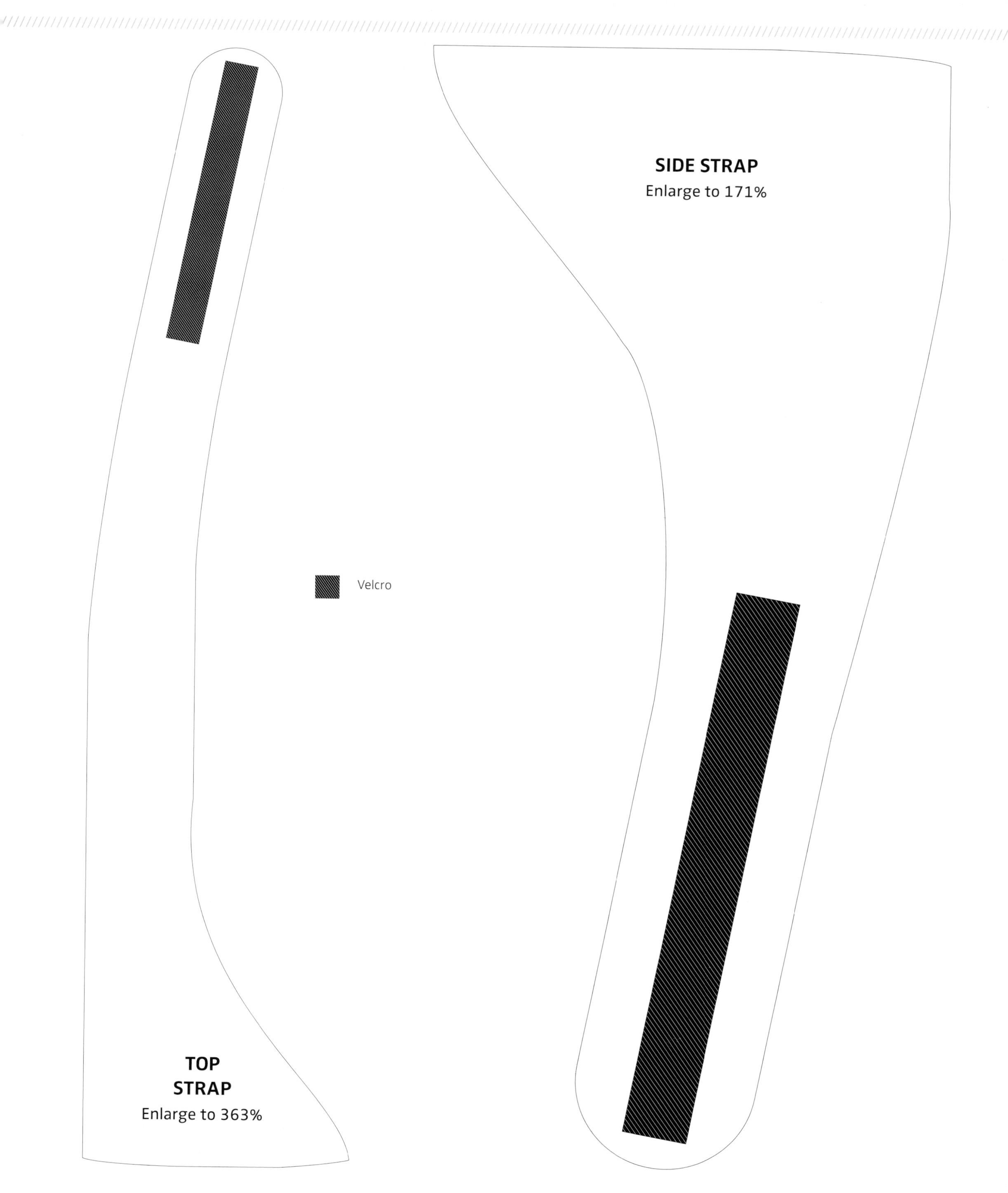
SIDE STRAP
Enlarge to 171%
Velcro
TOP
STRAP
Enlarge to 363%

Go bowling

page 124

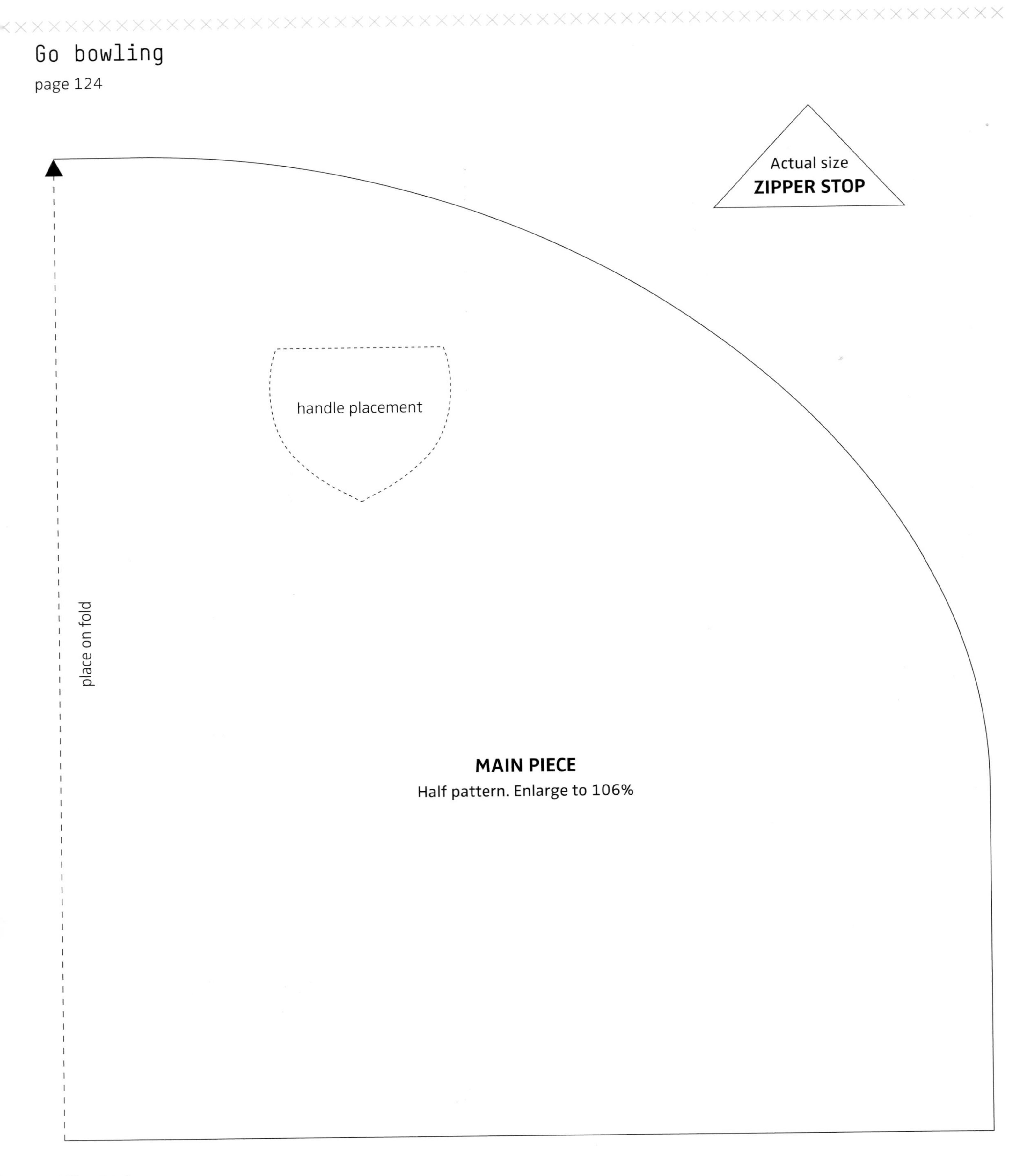

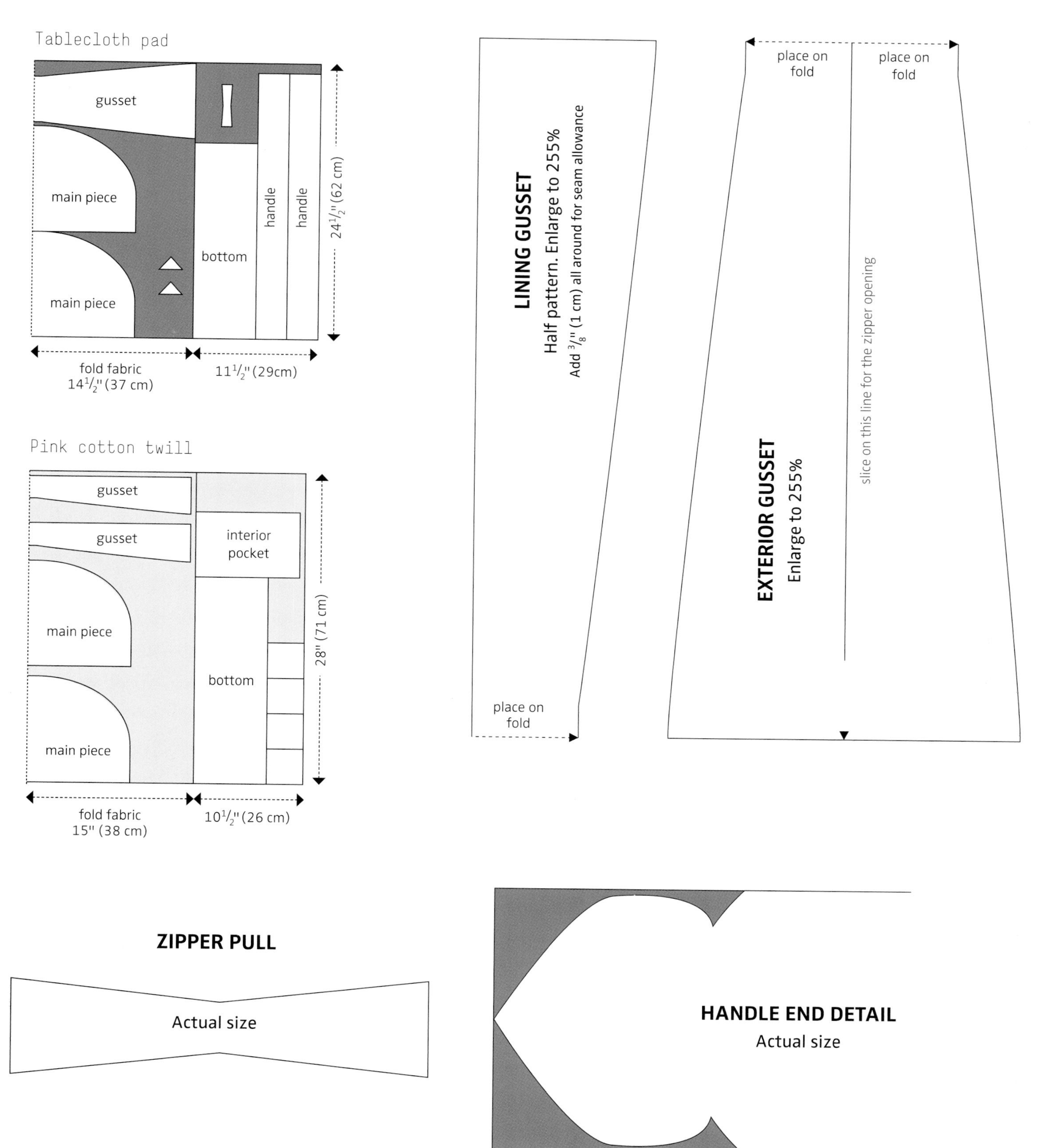
Tablecloth pad
gusset
main piece
main piece
bottom
handle
handle
24 1/2" (62 cm)
fold fabric
14 1/2" (37 cm)
11 1/2" (29cm)
Pink cotton twill
gusset
gusset
interior pocket
main piece
main piece
bottom
28" (71 cm)
fold fabric
15" (38 cm)
10 1/2" (26 cm)
LINING GUSSET
Half pattern. Enlarge to 255%
Add 3/8" (1 cm) all around for seam allowance
place on fold
place on fold
place on fold
slice on this line for the zipper opening
EXTERIOR GUSSET
Enlarge to 255%
ZIPPER PULL
Actual size
HANDLE END DETAIL
Actual size

Faux croco

page 130

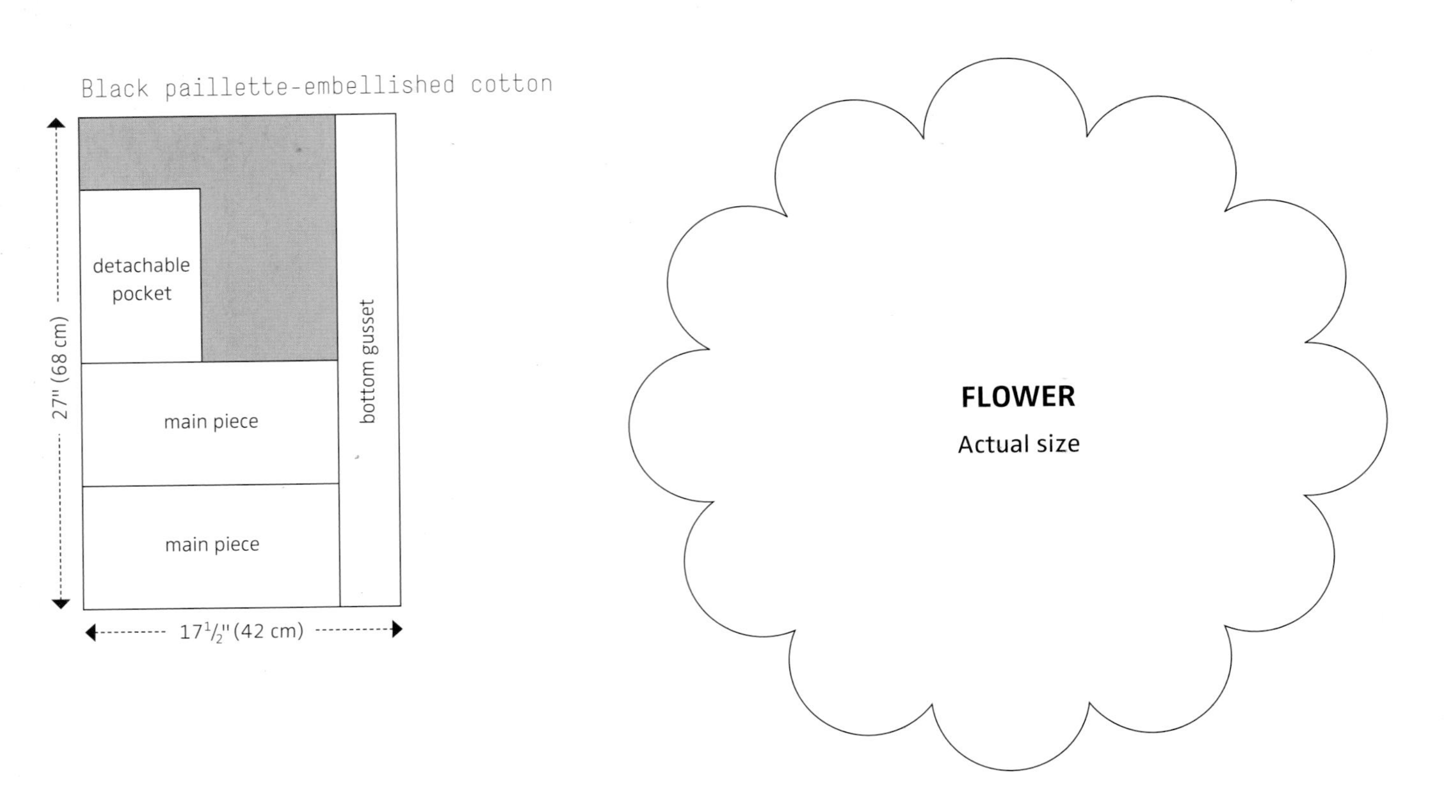

Black cotton twill

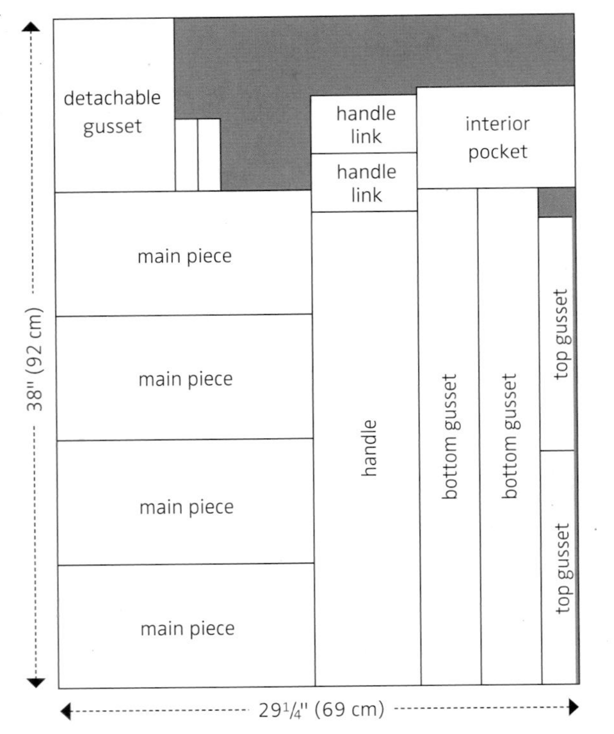

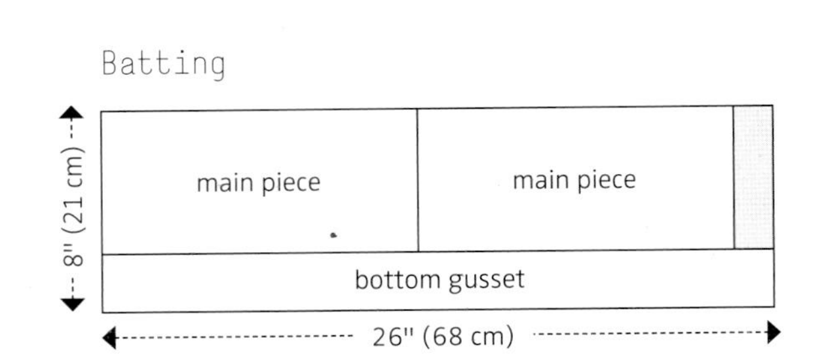